LEIGH ANDERSON-VOIGT

FIRST HOME
FOUNDATIONS

make buying your first home
simple, easy & fun!

I have never read such an intimate understanding of the problems first home buyers face coupled with a simple, easy to follow, step-by-step solution. This book should be compulsory reading for anyone wanting to buy their first home.

Tom Egan, Managing Director, Avia Homes

Before working with Leigh, we were pretty clueless about how best to break into the property market. But the wisdom from this book coupled with Leigh's hands-on guidance has been a total game-changer for us. Thanks to Leigh and his team, we've managed to buy two great properties in Brisbane. We can't recommend this book and First Home Specialists enough!

Rachel and Pep Karalus

Driven by a genuine desire to help, Leigh Anderson's *First Home Foundations* provides an invaluable, step-by-step guide for navigating the first home buying process with ease and confidence.

Kali Boermans, Director, Code Accounts Wealth Administration & Bookkeeping

Leigh is a unique and rare individual who has a desire to understand everything he does comprehensively. Equally impressive is his ability to then educate others in a succinct and easy to understand way on the topics he's mastered.

Tim Reed, Ironman 70.3 World Champion

Leigh's ability to combine amusing life stories while walking you through the first home buying process makes for an easy yet informative read. I was left with a greater sense of comfort as a prospective first home buyer.

Peter Crampton

If you think buying your first home is just a dream, then *First Home Foundations* is the key for your first home. From having the right mindset to how to put together an action plan covering all details, First Home Foundations is a step-by-step guide to making dreams come true.

Juan Torres

First published in 2024 by Leigh Anderson-Voigt

© 2024 Leigh Anderson-Voigt
The moral rights of the author have been asserted.

All rights reserved. Except as permitted under the *Australian Copyright Act 1968* (for example, a fair dealing for the purposes of study, research, criticism or review), no part of this book may be reproduced, stored in a retrieval system, communicated or transmitted in any form or by any means without prior written permission.

All inquiries should be made to the author.

A catalogue entry for this book is available from the National Library of Australia.

ISBN: 978-1-923007-55-0

Printed in Australia by Pegasus
Project management and text design by Publish Central
Cover design by Pipeline Design

Disclaimer
The material in this publication is of the nature of general comment only, and does not represent professional advice. It is not intended to provide specific guidance for particular circumstances and it should not be relied on as the basis for any decision to take action or not take action on any matter which it covers. Readers should obtain professional advice where appropriate, before making any such decision. To the maximum extent permitted by law, the author and associated entities and publisher disclaim all responsibility and liability to any person, arising directly or indirectly from any person taking or not taking action based on the information in this publication.

Contents

Foreword vii

Introduction 1

Chapter 1 Understanding the importance of strong foundations 7

Chapter 2 Affordability 29

Chapter 3 Preparation 59

Chapter 4 Network 89

Chapter 5 Support 109

Chapter 6 Build and style 123

Chapter 7 Looking towards the future 139

Conclusion 147

Acknowledgements 151

Foreword

There are two types of people in this world. You're either a Gonna, or a Doer. Leigh Anderson is most certainly a Doer.

Over the course of our decade-long friendship, I have been privileged to watch him set, achieve and then exceed everything he has committed to.

His business First Home Specialists (and consequently this book) is no different.

Leigh is one of the most disciplined, thorough, hardworking and determined people I am fortunate enough to know.

Everything he does is based on a solid foundation of research, critical thinking, analysis, and genuine, heartfelt care. He is a man of his word.

I have watched him pour tireless hours, days, nights and weekends into building the foundations and wisdoms outlined in this book to help as many people as he can.

Each time a new family gets a start on life in their dream home, I see it warm his heart. This is personal. This means something.

Even as a homeowner, I have read this book and made improvements to my financial situation.

You simply don't know what you don't know … until you do!

This book will help you. The ripple effect will be felt long after you put it down and store it away on a shelf – a shelf you own, in a home that's yours.

You can do this!

Kali Boermans
Director, Code Accounts Wealth Administration & Bookkeeping

Introduction

Building memories in a home you love.

Having worked with hundreds of young Australian families, it still never ceases to amaze me how buying a home can transform lives.

When you moved out of your parents' house or immigrated from overseas, you mostly likely found yourself in a rental property. Maybe even several rental properties! As time went on, you probably grew pretty sick of moving and having to ask permission for every little thing you did in the house. You want to put down roots and plan for the future. Getting married, having kids and buying your first home are in the top handful of great experiences you can have. Each is transformational, and marks a progression from one stage of life to the next. Turning the keys in the front door of your own home is about more than having just a house to live in. Owning your home makes a statement about who you are and what you stand for. It marks your first true step into adulthood and independence. You are king or queen of your castle, the master of your domain and maker of your life. You're making a commitment to yourself, to your partner and to your family. It's your flag in the ground. The property is the embodiment of your hard work, your dedication and your sacrifice.

Above all else, it's your home.

Over the years, I've founded several companies, among them First Home Specialists, Your Investment Group and Anderley Homes. I'm a former professional triathlete having won a silver medal representing Australia at the World Championships as well as being a former national triathlon champion. I worked as an executive for Telstra, overseeing 1100 staff in three countries, before beginning my career in property for one of Australia's largest and most well known property developers. In my property career, I have worked as a coach, a consultant, an investment strategist and a state manager. I have helped and advised thousands of clients to build a portfolio and create a legacy for their children through property. As well as owning my own home, I own a property investment portfolio spanning multiple states in Australia.

In 2019, I asked myself how I could take what I knew, which was property, investment, finance and high performance, and combine it with what I loved, being coaching, developing and inspiring people. And how could I use this combination to make the biggest impact in the world? It was this question that led to me starting my company – First Home Specialists.

My focus at First Home Specialists is helping clients with the transformative process of buying a first home. However, the most common thing I hear from my clients is the following:

> *'I want a place I can call my own but buying a home seems impossible.'*

I don't blame people for thinking buying their first home is impossible. Rents keep going up, property prices keep going up and the amount you need for a deposit keeps going up. For a lot of people, it can seem like they have no way out of renting. Most often, I see this leading to people getting frustrated and overwhelmed. They are often facing family and social pressure to buy a home, but they have no idea where to start. They're terrified of making a mistake, embarrassing themselves and losing their life savings in the process. This pressure freezes people into inaction and they get stuck in the unstable and unknown future of rental properties. In this situation, your home is not your own, and you have no security, no ownership and no permanence. It often leaves people feeling frustrated, hopeless and maybe even like a bit of a failure.

Fortunately, it doesn't have to be that way.

I want to inspire, educate, and enable you (and as many people as possible) to have the 'I can't believe we did it!' moment as you stand in the hallway of your brand new home for the very first time. I want you to experience disbelief as you walk around your house saying to your partner or family, 'I can't believe it's ours'. I want you to enjoy the pride of having your parents to your house for dinner; for your children to know the security and stability of a family home; for you to build long-lasting relationships in a community that is yours. I want your home to be your launching pad for your dreams and the aspirations of your family, and for you to create a future and a legacy for your children. People call it the 'great Australian dream' for a reason, and I want you and your family to experience it.

With the right knowledge, support and guidance, owning a home is not only possible, but also simple, easy and, most of all, fun!

In the world of real estate and finance, as a first home buyer you're often the forgotten and misunderstood participant. You can need more help than anyone else but few experts take the time to truly understand your unique needs and requirements. I work in the industry, so I understand why. Selling an investment property to a cashed-up developer is a lot easier and more profitable. It takes less effort to get a loan approved with a 20 per cent deposit. And the person buying their third home requires less explanation and less work than a person buying their first home.

All of that is true but, for me, nothing even comes close to the life-changing impact you can have on a person and their entire family when you make the seemingly impossible dream of their first home a reality. I've had clients in tears thanking me. Clients who won't stop referring their friends, family and anyone else they talk to.

I think our beautiful client Kasey summarised the feeling best with the following:

> Our first home has been life changing. I have lived in rentals since I was five years old. I've been able to give my children the gift of secure housing and a real home of their own. Our home is paradise. A big block backing onto bushland. A horse in the block behind us that the kids love to feed apples and carrots. Hundreds of corellas. Kangaroos at dawn.

Helping to create that is work worth doing.

Through this book, I outline my five-step First Home Buying System, which gets you from where you are right now and into a brand-new house and land package that you own. In the following chapters, I deep dive into each of the five steps:

- affordability (see chapter 2)
- preparation (chapter 3)
- getting the right network (chapter 4)
- how to get financial support (chapter 5)
- styling your home to match your personality (chapter 6).

While the steps in my First Home Buying System are linear and can and should be worked through one by one, they also work together. For example, a lot of the building and builder information found in the fifth step (Style) applies equally to the third step (Network). So I recommend reading through the book in its entirety before coming back to work through the steps individually. This way, you will have an overview of the process, understand all the moving parts and know how they integrate with each other before moving forward.

Before you jump into reading the book, I also recommend you complete my First Home Owner Scorecard. The scorecard will give you a first home readiness score benchmarked against each of the five foundations. To really help with your progress, complete the scorecard now and again once you've finished the book. You can find the scorecard here:

I'm on a mission to use this book and my First Home Buying System to create a revolution of first home buyers in Australia. My vision for the future is that the great Australian dream is kept alive for you, your children and every generation that follows.

Let me show you how.

Stay positive. Be determined.

Let's build memories in a home you love.

Leigh

CHAPTER 1
Understanding the importance of strong foundations

When you build a home, the foundations are the most important part. If the foundations are shaky, it doesn't matter what you put on top of them – the building is destined to crumble. I believe the same thinking applies to the home buying journey. Before you even think about buying a block of land and building a house, you've got to first make sure your foundations are solid.

Many people skip this important part. Most are so focused on the end result that they forget to get the basics right. I'm not just talking about the buyers either; I think most people in the real estate industry forget these basics as well. So in this chapter, I begin with the basics. Once you understand these basics, you can move on to the more practical elements of my five-step my First Home Buying System (covered in chapters 2 to 6).

In this chapter, I provide an overview of the home-buying process, and a crash course in the history of real estate and real estate trends. I then deal with one of the biggest determining factors in a successful first home purchase: mindset.

Making dreams a reality

Let me take you back in time. I'm 35 years old and in the form of my life. I'm in Melbourne working for one of Australia's largest developers. I love my job, I love my work colleagues and I'm making a killing in the process. I am living out my childhood dream of being a professional athlete and competing in triathlons around the world. I'm running at 5 per cent body fat and it takes me a full half hour to walk past a mirror. My life is the best it has ever been.

So you can imagine my surprise when I regain consciousness and I have no idea where I am or how I got there. I reach out and I'm surrounded by something; wait, no – I'm inside something. I push out with my arms and my legs and work out I'm in some sort of sack or bag. Then, without warning, whack! I'm struck by something or someone. Whack! I'm struck again, and I cry out in pain. I have no idea where I am or what's going on.

Next minute, I am in my bed, in my bedroom, in my house, safe and warm.

Before I have time to relax I find myself back in the sack again. Whack! Whack! I'm struck again and again from different directions. I'm trying to work out where I am, why I'm here and why I am having the living daylights kicked out of me. I try to think but I can't maintain a coherent thought. Every time I try to piece together how I ended up here, I'm struck again. And so it go goes, back and forth, between my bed and my torture. For the life of me, I can't work out what's going on. I'm terrified, and I can't escape.

As much as I can put thoughts together, what I assume is happening is that – for God knows what reason – I am in a bag somewhere getting beaten to within an inch of my life by God only knows who and each time I lose consciousness from the blows my mind takes me to my safe place, which is at home in my bed. I regain consciousness and get the life kicked out of me again, before losing consciousness and thinking I'm back in the bed.

Eventually I wake up, fully conscious, and I am back in my bed. I heave in the deep, gasping breaths of a drowning man. I sit up on the edge of my bed, in a lather of sweat and unable to catch my breath. I am terrified, I'm disorientated and I'm scared for my life. I get up and switch all the lights on. I look over at the clock – it's 2 am, the middle of the night. I'm traumatised, and I'm terrified that if I let go again I am going to be back in that bag somewhere getting the life beaten out of me. I can't shake the feeling – half an hour later, I'm still on the edge of my bed, body shaking, heart racing, breath heaving.

Eventually I turn off all the lights and try to go back to sleep, but the banging of my heart is keeping me awake. Eventually a thought occurs to me – and this one thought changes the course of my life forever.

If my life as I know it, right here and now, is an unconscious dream, it's the greatest and most detailed dream I've ever had in my life. If my friends, my life and my experiences are but a figment of my imagination – a coping mechanism for a horrible experience elsewhere – this is unbelievable.

But if that was the case, I wanted to see everything, I wanted to do everything and I wanted to experience it all. Most of all, I didn't want to not do things because I was scared. I'm not talking about the regular fear that we all talk about, such as being scared of snakes. The fear I'm talking about is the fear that sits deep inside – the fear that we hardly admit to ourselves, let alone anyone else. The fear that stops you from asking out that attractive someone, the fear that holds you back from taking risks like buying a home, the fear that stops you from living out your dreams. I resolved in that moment to do everything that I was scared of. That thought calmed me down and allowed me to peacefully drift off to sleep.

I awoke the next morning, the memory of the previous night's dream still strongly occupying my mind. I went about my life – I trained, I went to work, I cooked dinner – but all the while, I couldn't shake the feeling that everything I was experiencing wasn't real, that all of this was an unconscious dream. This went on for days and then for weeks; I just couldn't shake the feeling. I also couldn't shake the thought of the promise I had made to myself to run towards fear and to experience all of life. I couldn't remember if I'd made the following quote up or if I'd heard it somewhere, but this one mantra kept running through my head over and over:

On the other side of what scares you most is everything you ever wanted.

I then made one of the craziest decisions I have ever made.

On the basis of what was really just a nightmare (for me it was a profound experience but if we look at it objectively, I'd just had a very bad dream), I left my high-paying job. I left the security of my hometown. I left everything that made me safe and followed my dreams.

Nothing has ever been the same since.

That's how my company First Home Specialists started.

The book you're about to read, the journey I'm about to take you on is really all about how my dream is going to make your dream possible and I'm so excited to share it with you.

The home buying (and building) process

The steps to buying a house and land package can at first seem pretty simple. You find a block of land, design a home to fit it, get your finance approved and then have your solicitor facilitate the transfer. Simple.

As anyone who has bought and built their first home will tell you, nothing could be further from the truth. There is so much to know and, given this is one of the most significant purchases you'll ever make in your life, the stakes could not be higher. You then have the complications of being a first home buyer. I often describe getting a first home owner in to a home as being similar to a plane coming in to land. Very often the plane is coming in sideways, and you need to do a lot of work to correct the course before you attempt a safe landing.

Some of the more common questions or complications from a first home buyer include the following:

- What if I have a low deposit?
- What if I am a permanent resident or other visa holder?
- What if I have bad credit?
- What if I'm self-employed?
- What if I have previously been bankrupt?
- What if a family member is gifting me the deposit?

Believe it or not, with the right processes in place nearly all of these 'complications' can be corrected, and you can get in to your first home.

Throughout the following chapter, I take you on the journey and outline the steps you need to complete.

Before we jump in, however, you need to make sure your mindset is in the right place. My mantra for mindset has always been 'stay positive, be determined', and I explore the importance of mindset later in this chapter.

Once you've got your head in the right place, you can then move on to the five principles from my First Home Buying System – or, as I call them, the First Home Foundations. You need to understand and master these foundations to successfully move into your first property, and start building memories in a home you and your family love.

The following figure highlights these five foundations.

The five First Home Foundations

FIRST HOME SPECIALISTS
OUR 5 PRINCIPLES

01 AFFORDABILITY
02 PREPARATION
03 NETWORK
04 SUPPORT
05 STYLE

The five foundations work together as follows:
- **Affordability:** You need to make sure your dreams are realistic and attainable.
- **Preparation:** Before you talk to builders, brokers, banks or developers, you need to make sure your financial 'backyard' is cleaned up first – so you are in the best position to get your loan approved and move in your new home.
- **Network:** You'd perhaps be surprised at the number of people involved in a new home purchase, and your success is going to be determined by the team you assemble.
- **Support:** Here I'm talking about financial support, including options offered by the government. With the right financial support, you can bring your dream of getting in to a home forward by years.
- **Style:** This is the fun step, where you create a home that matches your personality and lifestyle.

Overarching all of this is your mentor. I cover mentors in more detail in chapter 4, but keep in mind from now that you'll need someone to keep you on track and light the right path to follow.

In all my time in property, I have never found someone who has mastered all of the five foundations and not ended up in their own home. Sometimes you need to think outside the box and sometimes the path is longer than you'd prefer, but if you are positive and determined you will always get there.

Property market overview

Real estate is the great pastime of Australians, we absolutely love it. In one way, shape or form everyone in the country is involved in it. There's a fair bet that today you woke up in a piece of real estate and tonight you'll probably go to bed in a piece of real estate. And the media can't get enough of the ups and downs of the property market. If someone wants to sell a newspaper or get an article clicked on, a sure-fire way to do it is to scare the daylights out of readers with a headline about impending doom in the real estate market. Interest rates are going up; property prices are about to crash! Any talk of a property crash makes me laugh – the entire time I've worked in this industry, the property market has been about to crash and all I've ever seen it do is go up and up.

Given that we're all exposed to real estate and we are bombarded with information about the property market, most of us assume we've got an 'educated' opinion on property (or, at the very least, we want to seem like we do). I believe partly due to our biology and partly due to the constant bombardment of media-driven negativity overwhelmingly those opinions are negative. It's hard not to get drawn in by it.

I remember when I first got started in real estate I was drawn in by the negativity. I was working for a major property developer in Melbourne. We were selling property in a place called Melton. If you don't know Melton, it's located about 50 kilometres from the inner city of Melbourne and is serviced by V/Line (the regional rail line of Victoria). The area has suffered a somewhat chequered history and has not necessarily enjoyed the greatest of reputations – not that I had ever been there to experience any of that. I had just heard it in the news and from family and friends.

It's fair to say I had some preconceived ideas about poor old Melton.

The developer I worked for had facts, figures and data supporting the impending boom of property prices in the area.

Infrastructure spend was confirmed and the state government had big plans for its future. Despite so much evidence to the contrary, however, I thought I knew better.

I was in the market for my first property, which was going to be an investment property, but I point-blank refused to be drawn in to Melton. Even though the options available were in my price range at the time, I didn't buy.

In the year that followed, I watched Melton properties double in value – in a year! I could not believe it. At the new doubled value, I could no longer afford to buy. The experience absolutely blew my mind, but also taught me a great lesson about real estate prices and opinions.

When the opportunity came shortly after to purchase a property in Adelaide with similar potential, I didn't blink. I literally bought it sight unseen, because I was not going to miss out a second time. That was my first property. I still own it today and it has been fantastic. It's one of my proudest achievements.

As one of my property mentors said to me over and over, 'There's only truth in numbers.' When it comes to real estate, I have never heard wiser words said.

If you want to know where real estate is going, you have to ignore opinions and look at the data. If you listen to opinions, you'll never get anywhere.

So what does the data say?

Over the past 50-plus years in real estate, three trends have been very clear:

1. Like an escalator, property prices have slowly and steadily gone up (with some sharp rises – see the following figure).
2. The average block size has reduced.

3. Affordability has moved outwards from the inner suburbs of the major cities.

In other words, you're now paying more money for a smaller block that is further out from the main cities.

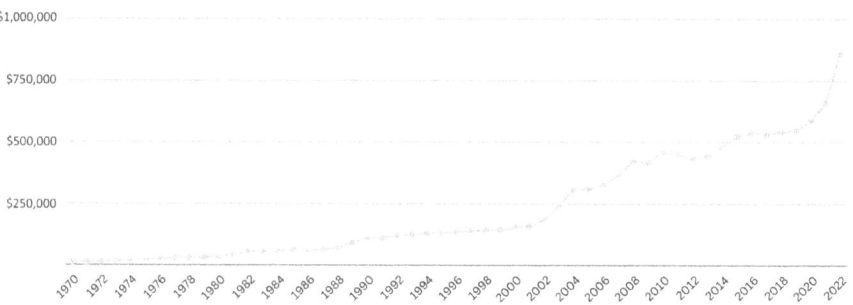

Average price, medium detached dwelling, AUD

You don't need to take my word for this – simply have a look around you. Think back to when you first left school or your earliest memories of property prices and block size. Compare it to where it is now. It's bananas, and it's not going to stop any time soon.

Why isn't it going to stop? Supply and demand. While the answer is surprisingly simple, the factors that influence these forces are complex.

Supply is driven by housing supply, which is basically the number of homes that are built in a year. A lot of factors influence the number of homes built, but the major contributors are the release of land and trade shortages.

Demand is driven by buyers. To understand this in more detail, imagine the property market as a pyramid. At the top of the pyramid are the mansions – owned by, say the Packers and the Rineharts – and at the bottom of the pyramid is the affordable housing (see following figure). While reduced demand is seen at the top of the pyramid, much demand is seen at the bottom.

Who is driving the demand? Principally, the following parties are trying to buy housing:

- first home buyers
- downsizers and upgraders
- investors
- self-managed super funds
- overseas buyers.

If the economy is performing poorly, the purchase habits of those towards the top of the pyramid will move down the pyramid to more affordable housing. This is the reason you have likely never seen any significant price decreases in the properties you as a first home buyer are trying to purchase. Demand always exists at the bottom of the pyramid.

The property market pyramid

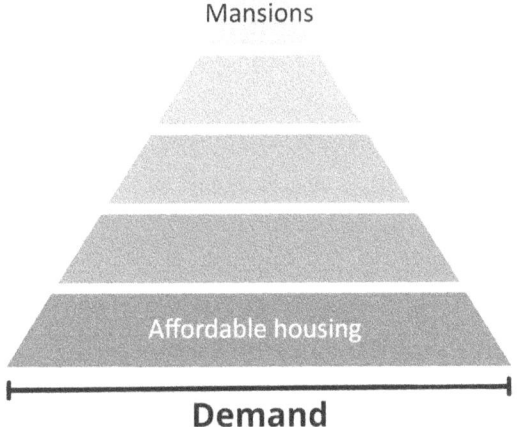

Recent property history

Now let's look at how general property market trends have been disrupted in recent years. At the time of writing this book, we have a genuine housing crisis on our hands. Not a media-driven beat-up of a crisis, an actual one. For the whole time I have worked in property, demand has slightly outstripped supply. This has been driven principally by population growth, which in turn is driven by births over deaths and immigration. Each year developers haven't quite built enough houses to meet the growing population in Australia, so prices have kept ratcheting up.

During the COVID pandemic, we also saw a property boom that was driven largely by the federal government's HomeBuilder stimulus package. An unusually high number of house and land sales occurred, which completely drained the supply of land. This led to some builders agreeing to fixed-price contracts to build on land that wouldn't be available for quite some time into the future. At the same time, there was a global supply chain shortage of materials, which caused the price of materials to skyrocket – if builders or developers could get materials at all. Many builders found themselves locked into a fixed-price contract where the material costs were greater than the contract price – and so builders all over the country started going bankrupt. It was an Armageddon like no-one in the building trade had seen before.

At the time of writing, prices have stabilised and the building trade is mostly back on track, albeit with fewer builders.

The government stimulus during COVID in part led to an inflation problem in Australia, which caused the Reserve Bank of Australia (RBA) board to renege on their promise to leave cash rates at record low levels, and to instead embark on the most rapid rates rise in history.

To keep it simple, the RBA cash rate has a direct impact on the interest rates a bank charges its clients, which then flows on to the cost of a mortgage.

The rate rises have slowed the property market overall. However, while falls have occurred at the top end, the affordable end of the market has seen prices remain stable or continue to slightly increase.

All of this government spending has left Australia with a whopping big bill that has to be paid. One of the main ways the federal government can pay this bill is to increase the amount of income tax collected – and the quickest way to increase the tax base is to increase the number workers paying tax.

How does the government do this? Immigration.

Australia's net migration for 2023 is on track at the time of writing for a record-setting 300,000 people.

Before this increase in immigration, however, Australia was already at a net housing deficit. This means even before the population lever was pulled, we already weren't building enough houses for the population. This is the reason both housing prices and rents are going through the roof – and why they're about to get a whole lot worse. What does this mean for you as a first home buyer?

Competition in the rental market is going to get worse, and the likely effect will be an increase in rents. Increased rents will mean an increasing number of people will realise they could be paying off their own home via a mortgage for the same price as their rent. The subsequent increased demand is sure to send property prices higher.

Block sizes will continue to get smaller as governments and councils are forced to allow smaller subdivisions and blocks to make up for the shortage of land supply. As an example, you can already see this happening in the city of Brisbane, with the building of secondary dwellings (or granny flats) by way of right now allowed.

Affordability will continue to move outwards from the main cities. Those places that seem far from the city now will become more expensive and less affordable, and home buyers will be forced farther and farther afield.

There's an old joke in real estate:

When is the best time to buy a property?

20 years ago.

When's the second best time

Any time you can.

I think never before in history has this been truer than right now.

Australia has less housing supply than ever, with reduced capacity to increase the number of homes built quickly due to fewer builders in the market, and fewer trades available for the builders that have survived.

Coupled with this is a perfect storm of demand just about to hit, with immigration at record levels.

After reading all of this, I wouldn't blame you if you said to yourself, 'Great, as if it wasn't hard enough already.' However, I also see this as an amazing opportunity. Traps for the unwary are out there, but if you follow the steps in this book, you will end up with a property – and a home. Right now, this idea may seem so far away as to be in fantasy land, but my experience and the experience of my clients is that property has the potential to set you and your family up for the rest of your life.

The home buyer journey

The home journey tends to be characterised by four distinctive stages, as shown in the following figure. Not everyone progresses through all of the stages and they are not always completed in order.

The home buyer journey

The four Fs

Before starting on our home buying journey, most of us live with our parents. Living with our parents often sets the stage for many of the attitudes and beliefs we take forward for the rest of our days. I was quite lucky in that both my parents, who are separated, owned their own homes. It was instilled in me from a very young age that you should own your home and that land is the commodity that increases in value. Unfortunately, not everyone was taught the basics to begin with – in fact, many people weren't. While starting to be corrected in curriculums across Australia now, I think it was a real breakdown in the education system that people weren't taught about money, debt and investing in school. While I got the basics from my parents, I wasn't truly taught the ins and outs of the property world until I began to work in the property industry. This first stage is characterised by low responsibility and complete dependence on someone else. Your home is only as secure as the people who own it. Your autonomy or ability to make independent decisions about the future of your housing is completely at the will of someone else.

Most but not all people then progress to renting. If this was you, no doubt renting was your first taste of the adult world – and of bills and responsibilities. To begin with, you likely had a great time, feeling like you had secured a piece of the world that you could decorate how you want. You could be as tidy or messy as you wanted, have friends over, and tell people to move in or out. You may have felt like you had your own little castle – that is, until the real king of the castle decided otherwise.

The ugly truth of renting is your home is not your own – you have no security, no ownership and no permanence. You commit to similar financial responsibilities as a mortgage, with very little of the upside. At any time, rents can go up, your home can be inspected or sold, or you could even be evicted. Renting is high on responsibility, but low on autonomy and security. It beats your parents place, but not always by much. For most people, renting is great for a little while but eventually the desire for a home to call their own kicks in. Given you're reading this book, I'm assuming that time is now for you.

Next on the home buyer journey is buying your first home. Your first home will probably be the hardest purchase you ever make. The property market is like an escalator, with prices slowly but relentlessly heading further up and out of reach. The hardest step you will ever make is getting on the escalator, but once you're on it's great. If property prices go up, amazing – your home has gone up in value. Given purchasing your first home is the subject of the rest of the book, I won't go in to the process too much here. Suffice to say, it will be one of the greatest achievements of your life and will always hold a special place in your heart. Your first home is characterised by high responsibility, high autonomy and high security.

Next on the journey come your subsequent homes. Most people's first home is not their 'forever home', although for some people it is.

For most people, their first home is a stepping stone. Their aim is to get their foot in the market, create stability for their family and then, some years down the track when their property has gone up in value, they will use the equity in this property to buy their forever home.

Equity is the value of your property minus the loan amount you owe. For example, if your property is worth $700,000 and your loan is $500,000, your equity would $200,000 ($700,000 minus $500,000). If your property value went up to $800,000 and you paid off your loan to $450,000, the equity in your property would increase to $350,000 ($800,000 minus $450,000). (This example is also shown in the following table.)

Property value	Loan amount	Equity
$700,000	$500,000	$200,000
$800,000	$450,000	$350,000

I explore this further later in the book, but the idea to keep in mind for now is that your subsequent homes tend to be characterised by low to medium responsibility, high autonomy and high security, mainly due to you earning more money relative to your loan amount later in life.

Finally on the buyer journey are investment properties. Investment properties are not for everyone, but they are the completion of the circle, where you create a home for someone starting out just like you did. They also provide generational security and a legacy for you and, most importantly, your family. Some people begin their home buying journey at investment (as I did) and use this to leverage in to their first home. Although covering investment properties in detail is beyond the scope of this book, I touch on how to use them as leverage for your first home in later chapters. Investments are characterised by low to medium responsibility, very high autonomy and generational security.

While not every journey is the same, the steps are predictable, the obstacles are predictable and, most importantly, the solutions are predictable.

Stay positive. Be determined.

As you think, so too shall you be.

I love this quote but it took me a lot of years to really understand it. So much of what we achieve in life is determined by attitude and our approach – by our mindset. I'll tell you a personal story that really drove this home for me.

A few years and about 20 kilos ago, I used to be a professional triathlete, competing in long-course events such as the iconic full Ironman event. An Ironman triathlon is arguably the hardest one-day event on the planet, consisting of a 3.8-kilometre swim, 180-kilometre bike ride and a 42.2-kilometre run. For the best in the world, the race takes just under 8 hours; for everyone else, it's typically 12 to 16 hours.

Believe it or not, it was my dream as a young fella to become a professional among these maniacs. After many years of blood, sweat and tears, I finally made it to the professional ranks. My transition from amateur to pro was characterised by regular humbling by more seasoned professionals. I never missed a top 10, but I was never really in the mix.

Possibly the biggest issue lay between my ears. The people I was racing, while now my peers, were previously my idols. The imposter monster in my mind had taken over. No matter how much evidence there was to the contrary, I simply didn't think I belonged – and my results reflected it.

It would be two and a half years into my professional career before I finally broke through this self-imposed barrier. This breakthrough occurred during the national short course championships. (A 'short course' triathlon still goes for just under 2 hours!) I had a solid swim and was in great form on the bike. I managed to break clear of the field and began the run with a small but healthy lead. It was only the second time I had ever led a race heading into the run.

As I started the run in a world of pain from the bike ride, I started rationalising my position and eventual loss. I wasn't the strongest runner; if I could just hold on to this pace, I should manage to come in second or third and still hold on to the podium. And so it began to play out. The field began to catch up.

Then a thought occurred to me: *Why the hell shouldn't I win this?* I trained harder than anyone else, I wanted it more than anyone else – why am I accepting excuses? With this thought, I went deep into the hurt locker and pulled out one of the best runs of my career. I went on to win the race and become national champion.

The purpose of this story isn't just to brag about being yesterday's hero. For me, I also gained a hugely important lesson about mindset in this race.

Often, I hear from clients that nothing ever works out, and they will probably get declined in their loan application; I hear them making excuses before we have even begun. It's like they are willing their worst nightmares into existence.

If you think things aren't going to work out, they probably won't. Similarly, if you think they will work out, there is a good chance that will happen.

Setbacks, disappointments and hurdles happen to everyone. What determines your success is not if you encounter adversity, but what you do when you encounter it.

Case study: Steve

One of my favourite clients, Steve, encapsulates this never say die attitude perfectly. When I met Steve, he was like so many first home buyers – slightly excited by the possibility of getting a home, terrified of the unknown and completely overwhelmed by the seemingly insurmountable mountain ahead of him. What made it even harder was he was doing it on his own.

I have the world of respect for all first home buyers but particularly those who purchase on their own, probably because I can identify with it. I bought my first three houses on my own and it was terrifying. You have no-one to bounce anything off and no-one to fall back on if things go wrong. It takes a lot of guts for anyone to buy their first home but particularly a solo purchaser.

Steve brought his brother to the meeting and after many, many questions decided to proceed. During Steve's finance application, the banks changed some of their policies (that is, the rules they use to decide if they will lend someone money) and he was deemed as being no longer able to service the loan. ('Servicing the loan' is a term banks use when they look at your expenses and your projected outgoings to decide if they feel you can afford (service) the loan. See chapter 3 for more on this.)

Steve was understandably devastated but in true 'stay positive, be determined' style, we put our thinking hats on and looked for a solution. The issue was servicing, so what we needed was more income. Steve couldn't earn more at his current job and couldn't really cut back on his expenses, so the only answer was going to be to find someone with an income who could go in on the purchase with him. Steve's best mate Sean also wanted to buy a home but didn't have enough income either. The friends decided to complete the purchase together, got their loan approved and moved in to their brand new home.

As a quick exercise, grab a pen and paper and draw a line down the middle of the page. (If you prefer, grab whatever device you have handy.) On the left side of the page or document, write down all the limiting beliefs that you have about buying property. When you think of getting into your own home, what negative thoughts stop you? Maybe you think you won't be approved, maybe it seems too hard, maybe you assume someone will rip you off, or maybe you say nothing ever works out for you. Whatever your limiting beliefs, write everything down.

Now start to think differently. What if everything just worked out? Ask yourself: would that be okay with you?

Close your eyes for a moment and imagine a world where everything just fell into place for you. Imagine how you would feel walking in the front door of a home you own. Imagine your kids playing in the backyard, and picture summer dinners around the kitchen table.

Now I want you to go back to your list of limiting thoughts and replace each limiting thought with a positive thought.

Next time your imposter monster steps in with a limiting thought, think back to your list and replace it with your positive thought. You deserve it.

Remember – 80 per cent of your outcomes are determined between your ears.

As you think, so too shall you be.

Stay positive. Be determined.

KEY TAKEAWAYS

- On the other side of what scares you most is everything you ever wanted.
- The five first home foundations are affordability, preparation, network, support and style.
- Historically, the three trends in property are prices increase, block sizes get smaller and affordability moves outwards.
- When demand outstrips supply, property prices go up.
- There's only truth in numbers.
- The best time to buy a property is 20 years ago – and the second best time is anytime you can.
- Each step in the home buyer journey leads to greater security for you and your family.
- When considering mindset, 80 per cent of your outcomes are determined between your ears.
- Stay positive. Be determined.

CHAPTER 2
Affordability

Affordability is the first of my five foundations for turning your dream of a first home in to reality. To use a sporting analogy, this stage is similar to the pre-season. No-one will really see or know about the work you do now, but it's going to make all the difference when it comes to game day. I find this early foundational work is what most people miss. When they decide they want a home, most people begin their journey with an online search on realestate.com.au or domain.com.au. While being able to visualise the end result of what you're after is important for motivation, you need make sure you are ready first.

Without a thorough consideration of affordability, this is also the stage where I see the largest number of first home buyers make decisions that end up locking them out of the property market forever. The essence of affordability is ensuring your goals are realistic and attainable. Unrealistic dreams remain just that, dreams. And the bigger your first home dream, the harder it's going to be to obtain. Remember – your first home won't necessarily be your forever home, but it is your step on to the property market. To achieve that step, you need to have foundational knowledge about the real estate market, what sort of property you should look to purchase and the reasons why.

In this chapter, I spend some time outlining realistic goal setting, how to think long term to get your dream home, the pitfalls of unrealistic dreams and the best type of property to bring your dream of owning your own home forward by years. This information will help you determine what type of house to buy and why to buy it, as well as the rough budget you are working with.

Setting realistic short-term and long-term goals

First home buyers often start with champagne taste – only to discover they are on a beer budget. I often see first home buyers with lofty goals for their dream home – and I love their passion – but what people often don't realise is how much a dream home costs. In working out your affordability, you need to look at two basic areas:

- How much can you borrow?
- How much are you prepared to repay?

The following table shows the required weekly repayments on a home loan at different interest rates and loan value over a 30-year term.

Now it's not all bad news with these repayments. Repayments are made up of what is called 'principle' and also 'interest'. Interest is the fee the bank charges you to lend you the money; not dissimilar to rent, it is dead money. Principle, however, is the amount you are paying off the loan by. A good way to think of paying the principle is it is a forced savings plan. You are paying off the home until one day you will own it. That money is still yours; it's just tied

Weekly repayments matrix

Interest rate

Loan value	3.50%	4.00%	4.50%	5.00%	5.50%	6.00%	6.50%	7.00%	7.50%
$550,000	$570	$606	$643	$681	$720	$760	$802	$844	$887
$600,000	$621	$661	$701	$743	$786	$830	$875	$921	$968
$650,000	$673	$716	$760	$805	$851	$899	$947	$997	$1048
$700,000	$725	$771	$818	$867	$917	$968	$1020	$1074	$1129
$750,000	$777	$826	$876	$928	$982	$1037	$1093	$1151	$1209
$800,000	$828	$881	$935	$990	$1048	$1106	$1666	$1227	$1290

up in the home. If you ever choose to sell the home, you will get all of that money back plus however much you have made with the home going up in value over time. I find the mistake some people make when looking at repayments is they think of it all as dead money, which is not the case. If you are currently paying $550 a week rent and saving $200 per week towards your deposit and you buy a home where your repayments are $750 per week, you're actually in the same – or better – position.

Another issue for a lot of people is looking at the potential repayments and realising they can't afford their dream home. I often hear people utter the following dream-shattering words:

Babe, I think we might wait for a while and ...
... save a bigger deposit.
... wait for prices to come down.
... see what interest rates do.
... try to earn more money.
That way we can ...
... get a bigger house.
... buy in a better area.
... find a larger block.
... get a better interest rate.

Saying these words, or similar variations, is the single biggest mistake aspiring first home buyers make.

The consequences of this could not be more serious.

Delaying a decision to get in to your first home has only two possible outcomes.

1. **Best-case scenario:** You will pay more money for a smaller house on a smaller block further away from your preferred location.

2. **Worst-case scenario:** You will never be able to afford to buy a home.

I cover the reasons for these possible outcomes in chapter 1, but they're worth a quick repeat here.

The past 50 years have seen three very clear trends in real estate:
1. Prices go up.
2. Block sizes go down.
3. Affordability moves outwards.

In other words, you pay more money for a smaller block further away.

At the time of writing, three other trends are making it even harder for first home buyers:
1. Rents are going up by over 10 per cent per annum.
2. Interest rates are going up.
3. Inflation is running rampant.

This means that it's costing more to live, it's harder than ever to save a deposit and the amount you are able to borrow is going down.

As I also discussed in chapter 1, building approvals are down and immigration is up. This means more people will be vying for fewer properties in both the rental and purchase markets, which will put further pressure on both rents and house prices.

This is why I joke that the best time to buy property is 20 years ago and the second best time is anytime you can. You don't know when or if you will be able to buy property in the future.

Case study: Tim and Courtney

Tim and Courtney came to us in 2021. They were your stock standard, run of the mill first home buyers. Tim worked as a tradie, and Courtney was a hairdresser. Courtney had recently become pregnant and they wanted security and permanence for their growing family. They wanted to live in Greenbank, southwest of Brisbane, and we found them a block in a beautiful master planned estate right next to a park. As often happens during the finance process, Tim and Courtney started to get nervous. They questioned whether the block was big enough, and whether they could get something larger. They were limited by borrowing capacity and this was the biggest block they were going to get in their desired area. Against our advice they decided to hold off so they could save a bigger deposit. Given it was income not deposit that was their limiting factor, this was never going to work; however, their minds were made up. They came back to us a year later and, to their credit, they had a bigger deposit. They also had a newborn child, Courtney wasn't working and in the year they spent saving, property prices had gone up by over 25 per cent! Eventually, we were able to get them in to a home but it wasn't easy and quite a few compromises needed to be made. They had to move to a suburb which was 20 minutes' drive further away, Courtney had to go back to work so we could get them a loan and they ended up paying $100,000 more for a block that was the same size as what they'd originally been looking at.

Does this mean you can't have your dream home? Of course not – I want to help you to get your dream home! However, you are going to need to start thinking long term if you want to get it. Your dream car might be a Lamborghini, but you likely understand that won't be your first car. It's something you need to build up to. The same type of thinking applies to your first home. You need to set realistic goals for the short term to take that first step.

Is it worth buying a home?

> If we have data, let's look at the data. If all we have are opinions, then let's go with mine.

Would you prefer to pay off your mortgage or someone else's? For most people, the former is the obvious answer.

Who wants to live in someone else's house, having to ask permission to put a picture on the wall, have strangers 'inspecting' their personal possessions potentially every three months, having their rent increased with little notice – and all the while knowing that at any moment the owner may sell and they will have nowhere to live?

You're reading this book so I think I can pretty safely assume that you'd like to own your own home.

The question is, is it worth it?

To answer this, we need to look at some specific figures and get our data nerd on.

Let's look at the following example. Say you're considering whether you should buy a property for $595,000 or rent that same property for $550 per week. In this situation, is buying the property worth it?

Let's take a look at the costs. Total costs for renting include rent and that's it. It's one of the benefits of renting. Unfortunately, however, rents increase.

Over the last 50 years, rents have increased at roughly 2 per cent above inflation. Since the RBA's long-term inflation target is 2 per cent to 3 per cent, let's assume inflation will average 2.5 per cent in the future, meaning rental increases will be 4.5 per cent. (At the time of writing, both rent and inflation are much higher than this, but I've taken the long-term view.) The following table outlines how the weekly rent of $550 will increase over the next ten years.

Weekly and annual rent increases at 4.5 per cent increase

Current rent	Weekly	Annual
Year 1	$550	$28,600
Year 2	$575	$29,887
Year 3	$601	$31,232
Year 4	$628	$32,637
Year 5	$656	$34,106
Year 6	$685	$35,641
Year 7	$716	$37,245
Year 8	$748	$38,921
Year 9	$782	$40,672
Year 10	$817	$42,502
Total rent paid		**$351,443**

As shown, the total cost of renting over the ten-year period is $351,433.

Now let's look at buying the property. Owning a house comes with more costs, including purchase costs, council rates, insurance and mortgage repayments.

Purchase costs include stamp duty, legal costs, transfer fees and lenders mortgage insurance. On a $595,000 purchase assuming a 95 per cent loan to value ratio and after deducting the first home owners grant (see chapter 5 for more on this grant) these are estimated at $38,000. Council rates and insurance are estimated to be $3,000 per year. For the purpose of this example, let's assume a flat interest rate of 4.5 per cent for the mortgage repayments on the $560,000 loan. Obviously, interest rates will not remain the same over the next 10 years and to be honest no-one knows what they will be. This is a weakness in the discussion, but we must pick a number, so 4.5 per cent it is.

The following table outlines these total costs over the ten-year period.

Total costs for buying a $595,000 home over ten years

	Annual	10 year
Purchase costs		$38,000
Rates and insurance	$3000	$30,000
Repayments	$34,087	$340,870
Total costs		**$408,870**

As shown, the cost over 10 years comes in $57,437 in favour of renting ($408,870 − $351,433). This is $5,743 per year or roughly $110 per week.

At first it would seem financially you are better off to keep renting. But dig a little deeper and you find more to the story.

Firstly, when you pay rent money, 100 per cent of that is dead money used by your landlord to pay off *their* mortgage.

As discussed in the previous section, when you make repayments on your home a percentage of the money pays interest, which is also dead money, but a percentage pays down your debt. When you resell the home, you get that money back. Almost like a forced savings plan.

In our example, the loan began at $560,500 but by the end of the 10 years the loan will be down to $468,764, meaning $91,736 of the loan has been paid off (as shown in the following table).

Loan balance after 10 years

Original loan	$560,500
10 year loan amount	$468,764
Paid off the loan	$91,736

Whereas before it seemed you would have been $57,431 better off renting, if you include the $91,736 paid off the loan you would actually be $34,305 better off from owning your own home ($91,736 − $57,431 = $34,305).

This hasn't even taken in to account the elephant in the room: compounding capital growth. Compounding growth can seem complicated, but put simply it is interest on interest. Let me give you an example, keeping the number round to make the maths easy. Let's say you make a 10 per cent annual return on $100,000.

$100,000 + 10 per cent = $110,000

So you've made $10,000.

You'd think at this rate of return, $10,000 per year, it would take 10 years to double your money by making an additional $100,000.

However, you would actually double your money in about 7.5 years, and the reason is compound interest.

As shown in the following table, in year 2 you haven't made $120,000 – like you would if you were only earning simple interest on the original investment. Instead, you've made $121,000. So where did the cheeky extra $1000 sneak in?

This is the compound growth.

In year 2, we don't calculate $110,000 + $10,000 = $120,000. We calculate $110,000 + 10 per cent = $121,000.

How this plays out over ten years in shown in the following table.

Compound 10 per cent growth on $100,000 over ten years

Start	$100,000
Year 1	$110,000
Year 2	$121,000
Year 3	$133,100
Year 4	$146,410
Year 5	$161,051
Year 6	$177,156
Year 7	$194,872
Year 8	$214,359
Year 9	$235,795
Year 10	$259,374

The gains shown are due to compound growth, and it is the secret to property wealth. Property goes up in value. Depending on whom you ask and where you look, you will get differing answers as to how much property goes up in value year by year, and that's because not all properties are created equal. Over the long term, houses have increased in value more than apartments and capital cities have increased more than regional areas. For the purpose of this example, let's assume the property will increase by 7 per cent compounding annually.

As shown in the following table, that means by the end of 10 years your $595,000 property would be worth $1,093,883.

Compound 7 per cent growth on $595,000 property over ten years

Purchase price	$595,000
Year 2	$636,650
Year 3	$681,216
Year 4	$728,901
Year 5	$779,924
Year 6	$834,518
Year 7	$892,935
Year 8	$955,440
Year 9	$1,022,321
Year 10	$1,093,883

With a $1,093,883 property value minus the $468,764 loan value, you would have equity of $625,119 in the property.

If you were to sell the property after 10 years, this means you could potentially make $625,119. Taking away the $408,870 costs of purchase and owning (council rates, insurance and mortgage repayments, as already outlined) equals $216,244. In other words, owning this property could make you $216,244 over 10 years.

Whereas renting a property could cost you −$351,422.

This means the financial difference between owning and renting in this example over 10 years is $567,666 in favour of owning.

So, is it worth buying a property?

Absolutely.

Rent money is DEBT money

When I was 18 years old, I got my first full-time corporate job. I wore a shirt, I had meetings about meetings, and I thought, talked and acted like I was a highflyer of the corporate world. (I actually worked in a call centre, but let's not focus on that.) What do you do when you've just made it? Well, I went out and got myself a credit card.

I asked for a $1000 limit. CBA, in their infinite wisdom, gave me a $3000 limit.

Armed with my new-found wealth, my underdeveloped prefrontal cortex and I hit the town. I maxed that card with the speed of a racing greyhound. I knew I would need to pay that money back. However, at the time, I didn't quite realise just how much extra the CBA wanted back on top.

It's fair to say my first experience with credit did not go well.

I swore from that point on I would take on no more debt. A man must know his weaknesses and access to money I hadn't yet earned seemed to be mine. It would be over a decade until I discovered a concept that would shift my thinking completely.

Rent money is *DEBT money*.

Think about it.

You must pay it – otherwise, you won't have a home. But, really, what you're paying is someone else's mortgage. And the amount you're paying is only going up. As already discussed, historically rents increase at about 4 per cent to 5 per cent per year. At the time of writing, rents are going up at a high double-digit rate, and they are not looking to stop anytime soon.

Compare this to a mortgage.

Part of what you pay is interest but part is the principle. As shown in the following figure, the proportion of the principle you're paying off with each repayment increases over the course of the loan. This means, over time, what you are actually paying off is a home that you will fully own.

Weekly repayments over time: proportion of principal versus interest

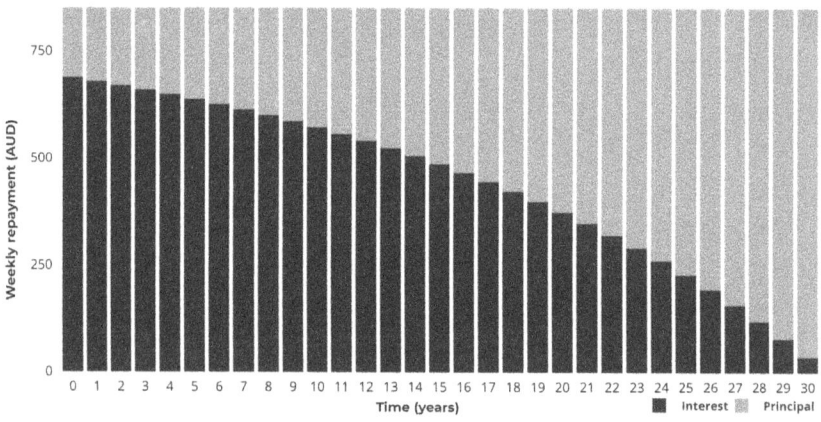

With your own home and home loan, you are in control. If you're concerned about your interest rates going up, you always have the option to lock them in using a fixed rate home loan, fixing in your repayment amount for up to five years. If you feel like your repayments are too high, you have the option of shopping around and refinancing to another bank. In fact, I would recommend doing so. Australian banks are far more aggressive in the pursuit of new customers than they are in their retention of existing customers. At least every two years, sit down with your mortgage broker and look at what you're paying compared to other opportunities in the market place. If your bank doesn't want to come to the party, you can leave them. Australian banks rely on existing clients' inertia and the Australian 'she'll be right, mate' attitude, which leads to clients never leaving. Forget that. Every bank has the same colour money – if you can get a better deal, go for it. (Remember to check all costs when working out if you can get a better deal elsewhere. While banks are no longer allowed charge exit fees, some discharge fees may still apply, especially if your loan is a fixed rate.)

Another important distinction I learned was good debt versus bad debt. Put simply, bad debt cost you money, whereas good debt makes you money. Some examples of bad debt are:

- credit cards
- Zip Pay, Afterpay and all other 'buy now, pay later' schemes
- car loans
- personal loans
- store cards or financing, even if it is 'interest free'.

All of these debts are consumer debts that have been used to purchase depreciating assets – that is, assets that are going down in value.

Good debts are debts that you use to buy an appreciating asset – that is, an asset that is going to go up in value. This kind of debt includes:

- property loans
- margin lending for shares.

I will agonise for ages about taking on bad debt and, even then, I will only take on this sort of debt where I could afford to pay for the purchase in cash but choose not to because I want to preserve my cash flow.

However, I will take on good debt with far less procrastination. I don't stress about my home loans (as long as I can afford to repay them) because I know I would be paying rent anyway and the amount of money I will make from the property will far outweigh any interest I have paid.

Once I'd paid off my first credit card blunder, I thought I was debt free while I was renting. I thought I was obligation free. What I realised was not only was I deeply indebted as a tenant, I was getting none of the benefits of being a homeowner. Empowered with this knowledge I bought my first home – relaxed and with confidence. My home has gone up in value quicker than I could have saved the same amount but, more importantly, the stability, friendships with my neighbours and sense of community it has given me have been worth more than money could ever buy.

Prove it to yourself – if you keep paying rent, how much will you be paying in 10 years' time?

The following table shows how much your current rent will be in 10 years' times if it increases at a rate of 5 per cent annually. In the 'Now' row, pick whichever amount is closest to your current rent, and then look at the amount directly below it to see what your weekly rent would likely be in 10 years' time.

Rent per week increased at 5 per cent per year

Now	$500	$550	$600	$650	$700	$750
Year 10	$814	$896	$977	$1059	$1140	$1222

If you bought a property, how much would you make over that same period?

The following table shows how much a property would be valued at in 10 years' time if it increases by 7 per cent compounding each year. In the 'Now' row, pick whichever property price is closest to your estimated purchase price and then look at the row directly below to see what your property could be valued at in 10 years' time.

Property price increase at 7 per cent

Now	$600,000	$650,000	$700,000	$750,000
Year 10	$1,180,291	$1,278,648	$1,377,006	$1,475,364
Equity	$580,291	$628,648	$677,006	$725,364

Rent is the worst kind of debt – it gives you no control, and no benefit.

You have all the pain and obligation of a mortgage, with none of the upside.

If you have to pay the money anyway, why wouldn't you pay off your mortgage rather than someone else's?

House, townhouse or apartment?

What you are buying is your home. This is the space where you will raise your family, where you will entertain your friends and where you will share life's ups and downs with the people you care about most. You will spend more time here than just about anywhere on Earth. The decision to purchase is, therefore, a highly emotional one – and so it should be.

You are also about to spend more money than you have likely ever spent on anything in your lifetime. Your purchase (and subsequent purchases, should you choose to go down that path) have the potential to set you and your partner up for life. Bought correctly and paid for in full, real estate can create security and a legacy for your children and grandchildren. The decision to purchase is, therefore, highly logical – and so it should be.

You no doubt see the conflict here. And, as just about any argument with your spouse will have told you, logical and emotional decisions go together like oil and water.

I would encourage you to try to be balanced between the logical and emotional when buying your first home, but with a lean towards long-term logical thinking.

So how do you do that? Here's some real estate 101.

When you buy a piece of real estate, what actually goes up in value is the land that sits beneath that real estate. A very simple general rule in property is that land goes up in value while buildings decrease in value. When thinking about the physical structure of your house, I want you to think of a car. Similar to driving a car out of the dealership, the second you take ownership of the home, it is going down in value – and it will continue to go down in value until one day it needs to be demolished. Like a car, the older it gets the more maintenance the property will require – and the more unexpected problems have the potential to arise. Old homes, like old cars, are unreliable and require quite a bit of upkeep.

When the price of a property goes up, the component of the purchase that is going up in value is the block of land that sits beneath the house. A large factor in the amount of capital growth (property price increase) you will experience is determined by the land component of your purchase.

If you buy a freestanding house on a freehold block of land, 50 per cent to 70 per cent or more of your purchase price is going to be the land. That means only 30 per cent to 50 per cent of what you have paid for is a depreciating asset – that is, the house.

If you buy a townhouse, between 20 per cent or 30 per cent of your purchase price is likely to be land, and the rest will be the deprecating house. This can mean a townhouse may not be the best investment.

If you purchase an apartment, the vast majority of your purchase price is for the building. You will not only be stung for body corporate fees and be subject to someone else's rules, but also have purchased a property the majority of which is going down in value. As one my mentors said to me, the only people who make money from apartments are developers.

Of course, you also have an emotional decision to make as well. Without knowing your individual circumstances, it's hard to pass comment on your considerations. Decide what aspects are priorities to you, overlay those with what is a wise financial decision and then push forward from there.

Case study: Mike and Jess

Recent clients Mike and Jess were a couple who had one child together. Mike also had children from a previous relationship who frequently stayed with them. It's fair to say that theirs was a busy household. Mike worked as a FIFO worker and Jess was a part-time teacher. They earned reasonable money and enjoyed life. What was important to them was space – they had a boat and jet ski they needed space to park and wanted a big yard for their kids to play in.

The issue for Mike and Jess was they had a low deposit. We worked out we would be able to get them in to a home but we needed to get them access to assistance programs such as the first home owners grant and the first home guarantee scheme in order to overcome the low deposit issue. Both of these grants have maximum purchase price limits applied to them. (See chapter 5 for more information on these financial support options.) The complication for Mike and Jess was the block size they wanted in Narangba, a north Brisbane suburb, was going to be out of their price range. To try to save enough deposit to not need the assistance programs was realistically going to take them at least three or four years, if not more. By that time, property prices would have gone up, leaving their home out of reach.

In weighing up their options, Mike and Jess needed to decide what was more important to them – location or block size and, therefore, lifestyle for them and their kids. They decided lifestyle was more important and made the decision to move to a suburb 25 minutes' drive away from their preferred location. In opening up their options in this way, we were able to get them a monster block with a huge house that had side access and more yard than you could poke a stick at for a cheaper price than what we were looking at for a smaller block and house in their first choice of suburb.

The preceding case study is a typical example of the weighing of priorities clients need to do when they buy their first home. A lot of my clients choose size and lifestyle over location, and I'm inclined to agree with them. Having moved around quite a bit in my life what I've found is you make a home wherever you end up. You always somehow manage to find your tribe and lay down roots.

New house or old house?

With unlimited funding I think most people would choose a brand new house over an old house. You get to select everything from the materials the house is built from, the location and the size of the rooms, to the colours, the façade and the overall style. Whatever your mind can envisage, your heart desires or your family wants can be brought to life in your new home.

Unfortunately, most of us don't have unlimited funding.

With the cost of a property becoming increasingly out of reach, and the pressure of the rental market closing in, settling for a second-hand home in your preferred location can seem tempting. At face value, this can seem like a reasonable option – older homes are often on larger blocks, in more established areas, and may even appear to be a cheaper alternative compared to a new build in the same location.

What people often overlook is the reason these homes are cheaper. To continue with the cars and homes analogy from earlier in this chapter, new cars and new houses are pretty low cost and low maintenance for the first 10 years. If a problem arises, everything is likely covered under warranty. Depending on the quality of the building, sometimes slowly, sometimes quickly, increasingly larger and more expensive problems arise that must be fixed and paid for. Ultimately, a car will end up in the junk heap and a house (over a longer time frame) will become a knockdown and rebuild for a developer. Used homes seem affordable on the front end but can be cripplingly costly on the back end.

This is partly why federal and state governments encourage first home buyers to purchase new properties. Across Australia, the state-based first home owner grants are only available on new properties. If you don't buy a new home as your first home, you miss out on these grants – in Queensland, for example, this would mean you forgo $15,000 worth of free money. You also get a significant discount on stamp duty when buying a new home, because you only pay stamp duty on the land component not the house and land. For example, say you bought a block of land in Brisbane for $300,000 and your building cost you $400,000. You would only pay stamp duty on the $300,000 land component, at a cost of $4,125. If you bought the same priced established home, you would pay $17,350 in stamp duty – a difference of $13,225. Add this to the $15,000 first home owner grant you are missing out on and you will need to save an additional $28,225 for your deposit and buying costs. (Your deposit and purchasing costs are the total amount of money you need to have saved to get a loan and buy a property. I cover this in more detail in the next chapter.)

New homes are covered under warranty – if something goes wrong, you can call up the builder and get it fixed for free. (In Queensland, all contractors are required to take out home warranty insurance through the Queensland Building and Construction Commission, so you're covered even if the builder later goes under.) Old homes, like old cars, are completely unknown. At best, you will have escalating maintenance costs; at worst, you could have a catastrophic problem that costs you tens of thousands of dollars to repair.

If you are considering an older home, it's worth working out what the real costs are going to be and if you are going to be able to afford it. Consider the following:

- What grants are you going to miss out on?
- How much extra will you pay in stamp duty?
- Will you miss out on lenders mortgage insurance waiver programs?
- What is the total amount of deposit and costs required to get into the home?
- What is the regular increased maintenance cost going to be?
- Do you have a significant cash buffer to pay for emergency repairs?
- How much longer will you need to save to make up that money?
- How much will property prices go up during that time and will that mean you need additional funds to cover the deposit and costs for the increased price?

The big mistake I see people make at this point is to say, 'We'll wait until we can afford a home in the area we want.' As discussed previously, making this choice invariably leads to you paying more money, for a smaller block, even further away from your preferred location than what you can afford now. At worst, you may find yourself priced out of the market completely.

When thinking about older properties, it's critical to consider the additional upfront cost, the ongoing and escalating maintenance costs, as well the requirement for a cash buffer for unexpected costs.

If you're not careful, what seems like a bargain can quickly turn into a money pit.

New homes cost less money overall, have more incentives attached, are designed to your specifications and don't have unforeseen expenses. It's for those reasons I recommend you purchase a new home.

Working out what's affordable

The best and most accurate way to know what property is affordable for you is to have a mortgage broker complete an assessment of your current financial situation. However, you can't get any old broker. You need to find a broker who specialises in first home buyers, understands new house and land and, most importantly, has a vested interest in your success. Finding such a broker is harder than you might think, and in chapter 4 I take you through detailed instructions for how to find them.

From the bank's point of view, when assessing what you can afford and whether they will give you a loan, your banker will look at three basic areas, which I call the three Bs:

- buyer (you)
- block (the land)
- building (your house)

These are also shown in the following figure.

The three Bs of finance

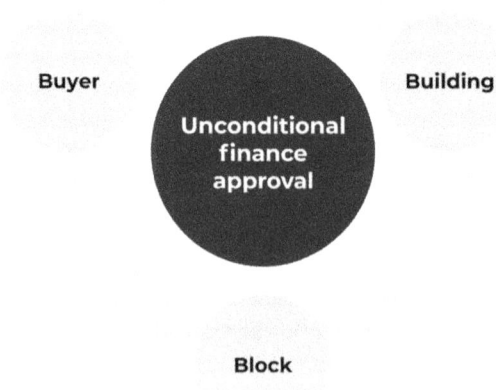

On the buyer side of this triangle, your broker will assess whether you can service the loan (looking at your income versus expenses), your credit history and whether you have enough to cover the required deposit and costs. All of these areas are influenced by a number of factors and all can be tweaked and adjusted, especially when you have a specialist broker and are aware of all your options. I provide much more detail on the buyer side of the three Bs in the next chapter. Before we get to this detail however, you can gain a reasonably accurate indication of what you can afford by jumping online and finding a mortgage servicing calculator. You have a whole host of options so pick your poison, but one that I think is reasonably easy to use is the St George mortgage calculator, which you can find here:

The following figure shows a mock-up of the calculator to give you an idea of the information you're required to provide.

Mortgage affordability calculator

About

We're Borrowing	By Myself / With Someone Else
Dependants Supported	− 0 +
Purpose of Property	To live in / Investment
Postcode	

Income

My salary before tax	Annually
The other borrower's salary before tax	Annually
Other rental income	Annually
Other income	Annually

Expenses

Basic/Standard Living Expenses	Monthly
Additional Expenses	Monthly
Investment Property Expenses (incl. Insurance)	Monthly
Current Home Loan Repayments	Monthly
Current Investment Home Loan Repayments	Monthly
Current Outstanding Personal Loan Repayments	Monthly
Total Credit Card and Overdraft Limits	$

Start Over | Calculate Borrowing Power

The following walks you through completing the St George mortgage calculator. (Other online calculators will have similar fields and requirements.) First select if you are borrowing by yourself or with someone else. If you have a spouse or are in a de facto relationship with someone who will be living with you in the house, you need to select 'With someone else' regardless of whose name the property is going to be in. (Basically, they're asking how many mouths there are to feed in the house.)

Next is the number of dependants supported, which is the number of children you have living with you full time. If you have 50/50 shared custody, some banks will take that percentage while others won't. (For example, if you have two children with 50/50 shared custody, the bank may count this as one child.) To be safe, put in the total number of children supported regardless of care arrangement.

The purpose of the property is to live in (not investment).

The postcode is that of the property you are looking to purchase.

Next add your salary before tax is deducted. Only include income that you can consistently prove – if you get paid sales commission or do overtime but this is inconsistent, for example, don't include this amount. If this additional income is consistent and you can provide evidence of its consistency, do include it. Don't exaggerate or under-estimate your income. Be as accurate as you can. If you are self-employed, include your taxable income from your notice of assessment. Most banks will take the average of the last two years although at the time of writing a few will only look at the most recent year. For almost all banks you will need to have had your ABN for at least two years and your tax return will need to be up to date.

To complete the other borrower's salary section utilise the same method just outlined.

Other rental income won't count unless you have investment properties.

In other income include payments such as the family tax benefit if you get it. If you have a side business, only include the income if you have had your ABN for two years or more and your tax returns are up to date.

Next, enter your basic/standard living expenses if you know them. If you don't at this stage, a short cut is to enter $1 and the calculator will automatically adjust these expenses to the minimum. Your result won't be entirely accurate but what you're looking for here is just a guide.

Leave the next few fields blank unless you have those expenses.

For any current outstanding personal loan repayments include the minimum repayment. If you are paying above the minimum that's great but you don't include that here. Make sure you include all loans here. If you have finance, the bank will find it so it's important to be accurate.

Finally include your credit card limits. If you have credit cards and they don't have anything owing and you would be prepared to close them in order to get the loan approved, don't include them. If you have a balance owing and you would be prepared to reduce your limit to the balance owing, enter the reduced amount. Contrary to what a lot of people think, having a credit card doesn't make it easier to get a loan. It makes it harder. Banks assume the card is maxed out and you are making repayments on the maxed amount, which increases your costs and therefore lowers the loan amount you can get.

Click submit and you'll get a number. Despite what the calculator says, this is not how much you can borrow. As a safe bet, reduce that number by $50,000. This will be far closer to your maximum borrow amount.

Let's say the calculator says you have a borrowing capacity of $720,000 – subtract $50,000 from that, leaving you with $670,000. This gives you a rough guide of what you can borrow. From the $670,000, next subtract $350,000 to $400,000 to build your house. You now have $270,000 to $320,000 for your land budget. Armed with this basic idea of what you might be able to afford, you can start looking at the real estate websites and start visualising where your first home might be. Head to realestate.com.au or domain.com.au, plug in your desired suburb, check 'land' in the filters and add your maximum purchase price, and now you have a map showing you the land that is within your budget.

As already mentioned, these types of online mortgage calculators provide a guide only. They don't provide an accurate number, but do give you a very quick and rough indication of what you may be able to do. You must talk to a licensed mortgage broker to get an accurate borrowing capacity.

Remember – if you find your borrowing capacity isn't high enough, you may be able to increase it. I discuss possible options in the next chapter.

KEY TAKEAWAYS

- Home loan repayments are like a forced savings plan.
- You're highly unlikely to be able to save money at the same rate as property goes up in value.
- The biggest mistake first home buyers make is waiting.
- Over the long term, you are financially worse off renting.
- Bad debt purchases liabilities that go down in value.
- Good debt purchases assets that go up in value.

- Land goes up in value, while buildings go down in value.
- Existing properties often cost more money upfront and ongoing.
- Book in to see a licensed mortgage broker to get an accurate idea of your borrowing capacity.

CHAPTER 3

Preparation

First impressions count and you only get one shot at them. This second foundation, Preparation, is all about making sure the world sees the very best version of you so you are in the best position to get your loan approved and move in to your new home.

In this chapter, I will take you through what it means to be finance ready, what an unconditional finance approval is and why it's the only thing you should be focused on. I also outline the three elements banks consider when giving you a loan, how your credit score impacts your loan and what you can do to improve it, as well as some tips and tricks for making sure you get your loan approved.

Finance ready

There's no romance without finance.

You can have everything else perfect – an amazing block in a suburb your family loves, and the home of your dreams filled with every inclusion you could imagine – but if you can't get finance, it will all count for nothing. Getting your first home loan is without a doubt the most challenging part of the process and in a lot of ways it should be your sole focus. The key to getting your finance approved is preparation. You should not be talking to builders, brokers, banks or developers until you are finance ready. Most of the problems first home buyers face are due to a lack of preparation, and that's mostly caused by not knowing what to prepare. With the right preparation, you will realise that buying a home is not only possible, but also simple, easy and fun. Preparation helps to eliminate any confusion and allows you to feel relaxed and confident when buying a home.

What being finance ready involves is knowing what the banks are going to look for, and systematically going through each of these elements to identify any problems. Basically, you want to see these problems before the bank does. If you can get to an issue before the bank sees it, you will often still be able to get your loan approved. If you try to fix the problem after the bank has seen the issue, however, you're unlikely to get your loan approved. They can't 'unsee' it and will often decline your loan.

Having too many finance applications is also a massive issue that can reduce your likelihood of getting your loan approved. Each time you apply for finance, that application goes on your credit file. Too many finance applications of your file may reduce your credit score and limit the number of banks you can apply to. Banks can also see who the application was with, when it was and how much it was for. If a bank sees that you've had three finance applications in the last month that have all been declined, they are going to start wondering what is wrong with you – and then they will go looking for it. None of us is perfect and if they look hard enough, they are likely going to find a reason to decline the loan.

It's much better to avoid this kind of scrutiny in the first place. In a perfect world you want to make one application to one bank that results in one approval.

I often compare getting a loan to dating. Not everyone is for you. If you don't get along with someone, it doesn't mean something is wrong with that person, it just means they're not your type of person. The same goes with banks – they have preferences too. Some banks love self-employed people, some banks don't want first home buyer business and other banks refuse to do construction loans. Different banks also have different credit score requirements. This is what's called their 'lending policy'. All the banks have specific policies and they are constantly changing. If you are not living and breathing that world every day, keeping up with these policies and the changes is almost impossible. And this is why I say you need a specialist mortgage broker. If first home, low deposit, house and land construction loans aren't the only thing your broker focuses on, they are likely not the right broker for you. It doesn't matter how good a broker says they are; you simply cannot keep up with all the policy changes of the banks unless you specialise. Brokers not knowing specific policies is why you can go to one broker and have them say they can't help you, but then go to another broker with exactly the same circumstances and have them say they will get you approved no problem. (Well, lack of knowledge and laziness, but that is a whole other subject that you shouldn't get me started on.)

At the heart of being finance ready is to first do an assessment of your current situation against all of the markers that a bank is going to look at. Next is to fix what you need to and what you can. I refer to this step as the 'finance ready plan'.

What banks look for when giving you a loan

A bank will look at three elements before approving your loan. I call these the three Bs: the buyer, the block of land and the building (see the following figure).

The three Bs of finance

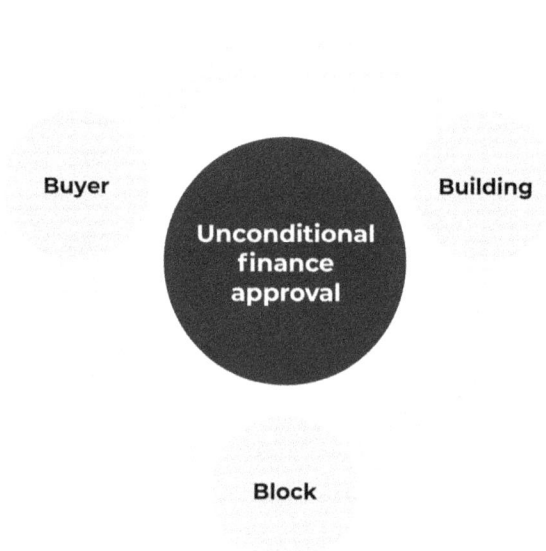

I cover some aspects of choosing your block of land in chapter 4, and cover building and style choices in chapter 6. In this chapter, I focus on what a bank looks at when considering you as the buyer. The bank is going to analyse three areas: your servicing, your credit history and your credit score.

If you are told you can't borrow or you can't borrow enough to buy the home you want, it will be for one or a combination of these three reasons. Find out what the reason is and fix it – and in the following sections in the chapters, I outline ways to do so. If the problem can't be fixed, make your goals more affordable so they fit your current reality. The key point I want to make at this early stage is don't accept no for an answer. Find out the reason, and then change your circumstances.

Again, as discussed in chapter 1, keeping a positive mindset is key, and an important lesson here comes from my time working as an executive for Telstra. I was taught this 15 years ago and I still apply and talk about it in my life today. The lesson was about above the line and below the line behaviour (see the following figure).

Above the line and below the line behaviour

Future-focused
Speaks with 'I', 'We', 'Us' and 'Together'
Practices personal responsibility
Positive and proactive

Above the line

Below the line

Dwells in the past
Speaks with 'You', 'Them' and 'They'
Habitually blames and gives exuses
Negative

People who linger below the line are negative people. They tend to focus on past events, and use words like 'them' and 'they'. Their mode of operation is blame, excuse, denial. They lack personal accountability and are generally downers to hang around with. You probably know someone who sits firmly in this category and style of communication. For me, being around these sorts of people is soul draining. I'm exhausted after dealing with them and I find I have to limit my exposure – otherwise, their stinky attitude rubs off on me. I find these people get the worst out of life because they expect the worst out of life and nothing ever changes because they never change. While it can be fun to whinge with them from time to time, it's not really the way I like to operate.

People above the line tend to be the go-getters of the world. They are positive and enthusiastic, future focused and take responsibility for things. They tend not to have problems – they have solutions. Everything in life is an opportunity for them to learn and grow. People and opportunities seem to be attracted to them. You can't help but get caught up in their positivity, it's infectious. I seek these people out. They energise and excite me, and I leave them with a renewed zest and vigour for life.

The reality of life is we all dip above and below the line. Life is not a constant. The trick is to self-monitor and regulate. If you drop below the line, you need to be able to pick yourself back up and get on with things.

I find this very true when it comes to buying your own house and nowhere is this more important than when it comes to finance.

So instead of giving up, I encourage you to put your problem solving hat on. You can always find a way to solve things and get you in to a home – if you're prepared to understand what limits you and think outside the box for solutions.

Case study: Susie and Aaron

Recent clients, Susie and Aaron, had originally signed on for a home in the west of Brisbane. Due to unforeseen circumstances, the registration on their block blew out. (Registration is when the land is confirmed as ready to be built on and can be purchased. Prior to that, the land is unregistered – think of it like an off the plan block sale.) Susie and Aaron were tight on finance to begin with, which is why they had chosen to purchase in an affordable suburb west of Brisbane.

The issue they had was interest rates were rising, and this was eroding their borrowing capacity. The likelihood was by the time the block was ready to be bought, they would no longer to be able to get a loan to pay for it. They made a difficult decision to exit the contract. They put their problem solving hats on. Their number one priority was to get a home and they didn't really mind where it was. They decided to go for a new home in a suburb south of Brisbane. We signed on for the block and got their loan submitted as quickly as possible. Another interest rate rise happened in the meantime and the bank would not approve them for the full amount to get their property. The thinking hat went back on. The amount of extra income the bank needed was minimal, so Susie spoke with her employer and they agreed to give her an extra shift at work. We then spoke with the developer and they agreed to let Susie and Aaron stay on the block while we sorted the finance issue out. Two payslips later, we had them approved.

Remember – stay positive. Be determined.

Buyer considerations – servicing

In this section, I explore in detail what banks look at when assessing your ability to repay a loan and their likelihood of lending you money. It's important to note that bank policy and servicing requirements change on a daily basis. While the following can act as a guide for what banks look at, you need to work with a licenced mortgage broker who can assess this for you.

The first element a bank considers when looking at you as the buyer is whether you will be able to service (or pay for) the loan. This is calculated based on your income, debts and living expenses.

Income

First of all let's begin with income, which includes three main types:

1. employment income
2. self-employed income
3. government income.

Employment income

Employment income is broken down in to full-time, part-time and casual income.

Your income is then further broken down in to your base wage and variable wage (such as commissions, bonuses and overtime payments).

Most banks will accept 100 per cent of your full-time income. Ideally, you will not be in your probationary period at your current job; however, even if you are, provided you can show a working history within the industry without any significant breaks in employment over the previous 12 months, the banks are likely to adopt 100 per cent of this income. Full-time work for an employer tends to be the easiest route to a finance approval.

Part-time employment is similar to full-time employment in that, ideally, you're out of your probationary period. Again, if you are new to your job, the banks will want to see continuous employment history within the same industry. Banks tend to adopt 100 per cent of your base contracted hours – that is, your guaranteed hours per week. If you do additional hours, banks will want to see evidence that you are consistently getting those hours and will likely 'shade the income'. What this means is they will not use 100 per cent of the income when calculating your income for servicing purposes, and may instead only use 80 per cent of the additional income. The exact percentage will vary depending on what bank you use.

Casual employment is slightly more challenging. Most banks will want you to have been at your job for at least 12 months. A few banks will look at your income if you have been there for six months, and occasionally some banks will accept under six months. Those banks tend to be unicorns with very tough lending criteria. When calculating your income from casual employment, most banks will take your average weekly income and multiply it by 48 (to allow for four weeks of unpaid leave a year).

Every situation is different but being full-time at your job often makes getting your loan approved easier. Banks tend to see casual employment as volatile employment and are less likely to lend when compared with full-time employment. So if you are employed on a casual basis, explore whether switching to part- or full-time is an option.

Banks will also take into consideration variable income such as overtime, bonuses and sales commission; however, they will want to see a history of the payments. If you have been at your job for two years and you can show that you have consistently received bonus payments each year, they are far more likely to adopt that income as part of your servicing calculation. When they do adopt this income, most banks shade the variable income – often to 80 per cent, but it depends on the lender and their policy at the time. For industries where it is clearly established that the majority of income is variable (for example, nurses on shift work), banks are more likely to adopt 100 per cent of the income.

Self-employed income

Self-employed income is the most complicated and variable income type you can have. The lending policies of banks for self-employed people vary wildly and the degree of competence required from your broker is high. I recommend dealing with a specialist broker who works with self-employed people. The issue most frequently encountered is accountants working with self-employed clients are often trying to minimise their client's tax by reducing their taxable income. Unfortunately, most mainstream lenders look at your taxable income to assess your serviceability. You have some options to get around this, with some banks also considering retained earnings, depreciation add-backs and even declarations of income from your accountant.

The path forward for a self-employed person will vary greatly from case to case so my best advice is to find a broker who knows what they are doing.

Government payments

Family Tax Benefit payments are the most common source of income I see for clients from the government. Most banks will adopt 100 per cent of this income – which is great because it's tax-free income – but this decision will be based on the age of your children. Most banks will only accept this income for children aged up to 11. Although some rare banks have more relaxed policies – if you have one child who is six and another who is 12, for example, they will half the amount of family tax benefit they adopt as income.

For other government payments (such as disability pensions), banks are likely to adopt the income if you can prove to them that the payments are ongoing. For advice on your personal situation, talk to a licenced broker.

Child maintenance income will also be included. Ideally, the payments are made through the child support agency so you can prove they are ongoing and enforceable. In the event of a private agreement, some banks will adopt this provided you can show a history of consistent payments in to your bank account.

Expenses

Next the banks are going to look at your expenses, focusing on two types: your living expenses and your debts.

Living expenses

For your living expenses, banks will either adopt your declared living expenses or the HEM (household expenditure measure). HEM is a tool used by lenders to calculate your general living expenses, based on generic factors such as your location, the number of children you have, your marital status and your lifestyle. It utilises 600 data points from the Australian Bureau of Statistics (and is not without some controversy, but that is a conversation for another day). Banks will adopt whichever of the two is higher, your estimate or the HEM.

Some of the common living expenses a bank may ask you about include:

- children and pets (childcare, sports, tuition, pet expenses)
- clothing and personal care
- communication (internet, phone bill)
- education (public school costs or private school fees)
- entertainment and recreation
- food and groceries
- health and fitness
- house expenses (including rates, gas and electricity bills)
- insurance
- medical
- transport
- other regular outgoing expenses.

Given that your ability to service your loan is going to be calculated by comparing your incoming income and outgoing expenses, if you are able to reduce your outgoing expenses – and prove this via your bank statement – it is going to make it easier for you to get a loan.

Debts

Banks are then going to look at your debts and what your repayments are. The most common debts people have are HECS-HELP, credit cards, personal loans, car loans, buy now, pay later schemes and payday lending. I outline these debts and how banks are likely to view them in the following sections, but keep in mind this is not specific financial advice. You must talk to a licensed specialist mortgage broker before making any decisions. However, hopefully the following can give you an overview of what banks look at and, potentially, some strategies as to what you can do to put yourself in the best position to get a loan for your brand new home.

HECS-HELP

A HECS-HELP debt is what it is – it reduces the amount of post-tax money you receive, and the bank will take this into consideration when looking at your servicing.

Credit cards

Somewhere, someone started telling people they should get a credit card because it will establish a credit history and make it easier to get a loan. (I wonder if it wasn't a credit card company that started the rumour.)

Here is how credit cards actually work when you get a loan. Whatever your credit limit is, the bank will assume your card is maxed out and you have to make repayments on the balance. If your credit limit is $10,000 – and even if your balance is $0 – the bank will adopt a $10,000 debt when assessing your ability to get a home loan. My recommendation: if you have a credit card and you don't need it, cancel it.

Personal loans and car loans

If you have a personal or car loan, you will have a minimum monthly repayment for the loan, and the bank will take this in to account when assessing your ability to borrow money. A lot of people think they can roll their existing debts up in to the home loan. While this might be the case further down the track when you have equity in the property, it is not the case when you are initially applying for your home loan.

I find these loans are often what holds clients back from getting in to a home. If you find that's the case in your situation, consider the following:

- Can you stretch the loan out by a longer period to reduce your repayments? If you have two years left on your car loan, for example, and refinance it over a five-year period, this will reduce your repayments on the car and increase your ability to borrow for your home.

- Do you actually need the car you have? Cars are a horrible investment – they depreciate over time (go down in value) and cost a fortune. Most expensive cars are a bit of a flex to other people. If you really want to flex, invite them around to the house you just bought. I'd quicker downgrade my car and own my home than drive a flashy car but be stuck in rentals.

Buy now, pay later services

Whatever your limit is within any buy now, pay later type services you've signed up for will be taken in to consideration by the bank, regardless of what you owe. Again, you're much better not to use these services at all.

Payday lending

This type of lending is a massive red flag to banks, and my recommendation is to never ever use it. This type of lending implies that you're living pay cheque to pay cheque, and could be an indicator of a high propensity to default on a home loan. If they see this, most bank will run a mile – or, at best, are going to ask some very hard questions.

Buyer considerations – credit history

When assessing your ability to get a loan the next thing banks will look at is your credit history. They will do this primarily by looking at your credit report, although if you are using non-genuine savings (such as a gift of funds for your deposit from a family member), the bank may also look at your rental payment history from your real estate agent. (The reason they will consider rental history is because it is proof of the ability to save when you do not have savings. If you've missed rental payments, they may reject your loan on this basis, so it's important to ensure you make rent payments on time.)

Credit reports are created by credit reporting agencies, with the two most common companies in Australia being Equifax and illion. Lenders provide your credit information to these companies and then they house that information for a period of time. They generate an overall credit risk score based on your history, and banks use this information to ascertain if they will lend you money. Many banks have minimum requirements based on the credit scoring system – for example, some banks will not lend you money if you have a credit score below 550. So your credit score and your credit history is very important when getting your loan approved.

Factors that influence your score

It's actually a bit scary how much a credit reporting agency will know about you. They will often have your current address, your previous addresses as well as your residential history. If they see that you have moved house a lot of times, they will see this as instability in your living arrangements and this can potentially negatively affect your credit score.

They may have information about your employment history and, similar to your residential address history, if you have changed jobs numerous times this will look like instability of employment and may lead to a lower credit score.

They will also take in to account the age of your credit report. The age of the report is determined by the first time you applied for some sort of credit, which may have been a utility bill or traditional credit such as a credit card. If the credit report is new, the lack of credit history may lower your credit score. This is probably the only circumstance where the 'get a credit card to increase your credit score' theory has some merit. If you are young and you get a credit card, this will open your credit file. Provided you never miss payments, it will show a credit history. Personally, however, I'm still against credit cards. These days, you have better ways to open your credit account, such as getting a phone plan. I see too many people getting themselves in to trouble with credit card lending and then having to spend years digging their way out of it. Each to their own, but it's a solid no from me when it comes to credit cards.

Next, your credit report will have your credit history. Included in your credit history will be all current open credit accounts you have, as well as all credit accounts you have had for the past two years – in addition to all credit you have ever applied for, regardless of whether you have taken the credit!

Credit enquiries are where I see a lot of people destroy their credit score. Most people are completely unaware that when they ring a bank to see how much money they can get for a car loan, the bank is going to run a credit enquiry. If you shop around to a number of banks, a number of credit enquiries will be recorded. Having too many credit enquiries on your report will reduce your credit score dramatically, and those credit enquiries will stay on there for five years.

This is why we are so careful with clients' credit files. We will never submit a loan application unless we are near on 100 per cent sure it will go through. It's definitely a lot more work to go about it this way but it's in the best interest of our clients so it has to be done. Don't let people run credit enquiries without your knowledge.

The type and size of your credit enquiry is also going to influence your score. As mentioned, the worst type of credit is payday lending. Even if you never miss a repayment, this type of lending paints a picture of someone who is living pay cheque to pay cheque and is high likely to default on a loan. Run a mile from this sort of credit, because it will destroy your credit score. Different types of more traditional lending carry different risks – mortgages, credit cards, personal loans and store finance are all going to affect your credit score differently.

Your repayment history will also show up on your credit report. If you miss payments on utilities or loans, it will show up. A number of missed payments is a key indicator you are in financial trouble and are likely to default on a loan. This is very likely to push your credit score down and limit the number of lenders you can apply to. Lenders will ask questions about this and are likely to reject your loan on the basis of missed payments.

Finally, debt agreements, bankruptcies, credit defaults and judgements are the kryptonite of home loan approvals. They will kill any application dead in its tracks. If you have some sort of dispute with a lender about repayments, you can't just not pay them and pray it will go away. They will list the default and destroy your credit report in the process. The most common thing I see here is where relationships go bad – for example, the girlfriend has a loan in her name for a car the boyfriend is driving and he promises to make all the repayments on the loan. What the girlfriend often fails to realise is, although she doesn't drive the car and doesn't make the repayments, she is responsible for them. Any missed payments go on her credit report, not his. Where I see this go very bad is when the relationship goes sour. They split up, the loan is still in her name and he stops making the repayments – and she gets the default listed under her name because she is the responsible party. Her credit is then ruined for the next five years. The best course of action is to avoid this situation in its entirety. Do not get credit for other people.

Finding a home loan with a bad credit score

If you do find you have bad credit score of some description, it's not always game over. You can often find a way to still get a home loan; however, the degree of difficulty certainly goes up. You will need expert help and guidance to do this but the first place I would start would be to see if there is a way to get the default removed. On a case by case basis, this can sometimes happen. Failing that, some non-mainstream lenders out there will help people with credit issues. Generally in this situation, you are going to pay higher interest rates and fees for those lenders.

Case study: Nathan and Rachel

To give you an example of getting a default removed from your credit report, I'll tell you about two clients of mine, Nathan and Rachel. Nathan and Rach had two kids; Nathan was the major bread winner with Rach working part-time. They serviced well (that is, how much of a loan they could get based on their income and expenses) but everyone kept telling them they couldn't help. They were beside themselves. As part of our Finance Ready program that all clients go through before talking with brokers, banks or developers, we discovered Nathan had a default on his credit report. This default brought his credit score down to 270, which meant he couldn't get a loan anywhere. (Most banks require a minimum credit score of 550 to 600.)

Rather than saying no, we investigated the default. It turned out it was from a previous marriage and we believed it had incorrectly been put on his credit file. Our team negotiated with a lender on Nathan's behalf and got the default removed. This boosted his credit score up to 650, and we were able to get them a loan so they could start building memories in a home they loved.

This isn't an isolated incident. We see this all the time where a first home buyer, with the right preparation, can get a home when they had previously been told no.

Before approaching any lenders, you should get a hold of your credit file so you can see what they are seeing.

You can visit Equifax or illion using the following:

Buyer considerations – deposit and costs

The next thing the banks will look at when assessing the buyer element of getting a loan approved is the amount you have for deposit and costs. When most first home buyers think of a deposit, they forget about purchasing costs. In this section I break down typical deposit amounts and go through the typical costs a first home buyer will need to budget for.

Typically, a home buyer will have a 5, 10, 20 or 30 per cent deposit. The rest of the home will be purchased with a loan. A 5 per cent deposit is obviously the quickest and easiest to save up, but it comes with the most fees associated and will attract the highest interest rate by virtue of it being seen as a riskier loan by the banks. If you have a 30 per cent deposit, banks will practically fall over themselves trying to give you money – but you will probably be a grandparent before you are able to save up that much. As already discussed, most people can't save money at the same rate as property goes up in value. For most people, by the time they save what they'd budgeted as a 20 per cent deposit, property prices will have gone up at such a rate that their preferred property will now be out of reach, and they will need to look at a house on a smaller block, further away from their preference and which will cost them more. For this reason most first home buyers will look at the lowest deposit option. While it is not the most cost effective, it does get your foot in the door – which is the whole aim of the game.

Next we have purchasing costs, and these are often higher than many first home buyers expect. If you are attempting to purchase a property with a 5 per cent deposit, you will also need to save the 5 per cent plus enough to cover the additional costs. These fees can vary between lenders and depending on where (and the property type) you're purchasing but the following gives you a breakdown of what some of the associated costs may look like:

- Purchase price: $614,000.
- 5 per cent deposit: $30,700.
- Lenders mortgage insurance: $22,152.
- Legal fees: $1500.
- Transfer duty: $979.
- Stamp duty: $1140 (based on buying a new property).
- Bank fees: $500.

In this example, the total amount required to cover the deposit and costs is $56,971.

The bank won't lend you 100 per cent of the purchase amount, so the deposit makes up the amount they are not lending. In this example, the maximum loan amount is 95 per cent so the deposit makes up 5 per cent of the purchase. Given most people think they just need the 5 per cent, you're probably looking at this and saying to yourself, 'You're kidding me, aren't you?!' These costs pretty much double the deposit requirements.

Let me break down what all the fees are:

- **Lenders mortgage insurance:** This is the biggest kick in the teeth on a first home purchase. Banks see any lending over 80 per cent of the purchase price as risky, so they have the loan insured. The insurance covers the bank in the event you default on the loan. They then charge that insurance premium back to their clients. This means you pay for an insurance policy for the bank. If you default, you get nothing and the bank is covered. The fee for this insurance is high and all of the banks do it. Don't start me on how unfair I think this is but, unfortunately, if you want their money you need to play by their rules. Note that banks will charge the insurance for any deposit lower than 20 per cent. In the above example, even if you have a 10 per cent deposit, the lenders mortgage insurance would still be $13,593.

- **Legal fees:** When you purchase a block of land, the land needs to be transferred from the developer's name in to your name. In order to do this, your solicitor or conveyancer needs to talk to their solicitor to facilitate the transfer – and, of course, they'll charge you for this.

- **Transfer and stamp duty are government taxes:** As a first home buyer, you get a significantly discounted stamp duty

rate but in most cases the government still wants its pound of flesh. One of the benefits of purchasing a new property is you only pay stamp duty on the land component not the entire purchase price, which give you a significant saving.
- **Bank fees:** Banks all have various fees. Again, it's the unfortunate cost of doing business with them.

Saving a deposit is by far the hardest part of getting a home for first home buyers. It is such a big issue that I have dedicated an entire chapter (and foundation in our process) to getting you financial support so you can reduce your deposit and saving requirements – bringing your dreams forward potentially by years.

Bank approvals

You can get three types of loan approval from a bank.

The first is what's called a 'pre-approval' – most people have heard of this term and believe it is the first step toward getting a new home. I find a lot of first home buyers think a pre-approval is going to tell them how much they can borrow – and then they are able to go out and shop for a home based on that commitment from the bank. This is not correct. Pre-approvals are nice to have but, ultimately, they are useless. Let me explain why.

In the pre-approval process, banks only look at one of the three Bs introduced earlier in this chapter– the buyer. In order for you to get unconditionally approved, the bank is going to need to consider the other two elements – block and building. Banks will lend more money on bigger blocks, for example, and less money on 'ski slope' blocks. If a bank is over exposed to an area, they can often lend with a lower LVR or may not even lend at all. (LVR stands for loan to value ratio and is expressed as the opposite of deposit.

For example, if you have a 20 per cent deposit, this would be an 80 per cent loan to value ratio. In financial terms, if the property was valued at $1,000,000 and you had a $100,000 deposit, this would be a 10 per cent deposit or a 90 per cent loan to value ratio (LVR).) Banks also tend to lend more money for bigger buildings – they will lend more on a four-bedroom house than a three-bedroom townhouse, for example.

A preapproval goes through a full finance process based just on you. This means at a high level they will consider the three elements discussed in this chapter – your servicing potential, your credit history, and your deposit and costs requirements.

You can also get almost the equivalent to a pre-approval on all the information you need without ever talking to a bank. If your broker is a first home specialist and has a sound understanding of the banks and their lending policies, they should be able to gather all the required information, run it through the servicing calculators of the banks and get the same answer without ever having submitted a loan application. This gives you all the upside benefit of a pre-approval without any of the downside risk.

You also don't know if you are going to go with a specific bank yet, so why would you bother approaching them? Brokers who specialise in first home buyers all go through a similar process to the following. They will give you an indication of your budget during the preparation phase. Once you have a land and a build contract (signed 'subject to finance', which I cover in chapter 4), they will then look at their list of banks and bank policies and advise from there.

For example, let's say your broker begins with 35 different banks they could potentially use. Based on your circumstances, the block of land and the building you've chosen, they will immediately rule out 25 of those based on bank lending policy. This gives them a shortlist of 10 banks. All brokers have relationships with the business development managers (BDMs) at the banks. If the broker has your best interests at heart, rather than just submitting your loan application and hoping for the best, they will call their BDM and say something like, 'This is the customer I have, this is their block and this is the building we are putting on it. Do you think you would approve the loan?' Of the 10 banks the broker approached, maybe four will say no – great, it's much better to find out based on a conversation rather than an application. Maybe three will say something like, 'Yeah, maybe. Submit and see how you go.' This is terrible – you don't want to be submitting loans based on 'flip of a coin' outcomes. Then perhaps three banks will say that it looks like a deal for them, and they want the business. That's who you are looking for.

Remember – at this stage of the game, you are just looking for an approval; that's your only priority. The best interest rates in the world won't help you if the bank declines your application. A specialist broker should come back to you with a shortlist of options and make a recommendation based on which bank is most likely to approve you. The leap you are trying to make here – from being an unsecured creditor to a secured creditor – is one of the hardest you are going to make. Once you are a home owner, you will be amazed at how your lending profile changes and how easily you will be able to access credit compared to before. I'm not recommending you should get the credit, but it's incredible how many companies start throwing it at you once you are secured.

If you have followed the process just outlined, the broker will then submit your loan to the lender where you are most likely to get an approval.

Generally, the next step from here is to get a conditional approval – which is the bank saying, 'Yes, we've given this loan the sniff test and it looks good, but we need a few more supporting docs before we will formally approve the loan'.

Once they have those supporting documents, you will then be formally approved with an unconditional finance approval. This is what you need – this is the aim of the game when it comes to lending. It is an official agreement from the bank to lend you money for your first home. You can take this and go unconditional on your land and building contract and proceed with your purchase.

What to do if you can't buy a home

You may go through all the steps outlined in this Preparation foundation and find out you can't buy a home. At this point, a lot of people – in fact, most people – give up. They put the home buying issue in the too hard basket to be dealt with at some undetermined date in the future. I believe this is a mistake.

Firstly, it's not that you can't buy a home. What you have discovered is you can't buy your preferred home with your current circumstances. Below the line thinking (outlined earlier in this chapter) will have you tell yourself buying a home is impossible. 'This is unfair,' you may say. 'Why does this always happen to me?' In some ways, fair enough; I actually agree with you. It is a little bit unfair. There has never been a harder time in history for first home buyers to get in to the property market, and the people who make the rules determining whether or not you can purchase a property are so far removed from the real world struggles of first home buyers that they couldn't possibly understand the difficulties you are experiencing. This is all true – but it is not likely to change.

Above the line thinking would have you ask yourself, 'What can I do differently to change my circumstances?' This question is the essence of personal responsibility and success. As the famous psychologist and holocaust survivor Victor Frankl said:

Everything can be taken from a man but one thing: the last of the human freedoms – to choose one's attitude in any given set of circumstances, to choose one's own way.

You can't help what happens to you but you can change how you react to it – and this is why I say 'Stay positive. Be determined.' Where there is a will there is a way and to every problem there is a solution.

Your first step is to determine your limiting factor. It will either be your servicing potential, your credit history, or your deposit and costs requirements. Make sure you are specific when you find out the issue – the broad area isn't enough. Just knowing your credit score is too low doesn't help – knowing your credit score is 450 because of a Telstra credit default from three years ago is helpful. That's a problem you can work to fix.

Once you know your specific problem, you can work on specific solutions. For example, one of the more common hurdles I see in front of people is not being able to service a loan big enough to get in to the home they want. If you find yourself in this situation, ask yourself:

- Are you dreams affordable? Could you look at a cheaper house to begin with and then leapfrog into the bigger house a few years down the track?
- Do you have debt that you could either close or refinance to a lower repayment amount, reducing your outgoings and increasing your borrowings?
- Do you have any fixed expenditures that can be reduced, thereby increasing your borrowing potential? I've had clients

go as far as moving their kids to different schools to reduce school fees because they made a judgement call that having a permanent home was going to be better for their kids than them remaining at the same school but living in a rental.

- If your issue is income, do you have a job where you can pick up more shifts and earn more money? Could you get a second job?
- Is there another person who would be willing to go in on the house with you? I've had clients buy homes with friends, siblings and parents. If you can't do it on your own, partner up with someone in a similar situation.

If your issue is something in your credit file, you will probably need specialist support to fix this. Credit repair companies can look in to this for you.

If your issue is saving up the required amount to cover the deposit and costs, read chapter 5, where I go into detail on the possible financial support available.

Every problem can be overcome if you are prepared to put your solutions hat on and think outside the box.

Stay positive. Be determined.

10 things you can do to increase your chance of getting your loan approved

Want to know how to put yourself in the best position to get a home loan approved? Here are 10 tips and tricks:

1. **Save as much as you can:** The more you have in savings, the easier it is to get approved and the less you will have to pay in fees such as lenders mortgage insurance.

2. **Earn more money:** If you have a job where you can pick up extra shifts, do it. The more income you can show, the more likely you are to get approved.
3. **Don't apply for credit:** Not only will the additional interest repayments reduce your servicing, but each credit application (even if it is just an enquiry) goes on your credit file and may reduce your credit score, potentially limiting the number of banks you can apply to.
4. **Don't miss payments on rent and loans:** These may show up on your credit report or tenant history, reducing your likelihood of an approval.
5. **Don't create adverse credit history:** If you don't pay your utility bills, a company may list a default on your credit report – and you may not be able to get finance.
6. **Reduce unnecessary expenditure:** Your servicing potential or amount you can borrow is a product of your income versus your expenditure – the less you spend, the more you can borrow and the more likely you are to be approved.
7. **Reduce debt:** Lenders look at your debt-to-income ratio when assessing your loan application. Reduce your debt by paying off credit card balances and personal loans.
8. **Stay away from buy now, pay later options:** They are still classed as debt and will reduce the amount you can borrow.
9. **Have a squeaky clean bank statement:** Avoid overdrawn fees on all of your accounts and be mindful that your statements tell a story about you. If a lender sees multiple entries for Sportsbet or payday lenders, for example, they are going to start asking questions, which may reduce your likelihood of an approval.

10. **Don't change job or employment type:** Lenders look at employment history and this has a major impact on your ability to get approved. Some of the typical mistakes people make are going from full-time to casual, starting a new job for less money, or going from full-time or part-time to contract ABN work. If you need to change job, the best course of action is to talk to your broker before committing to any changes.

KEY TAKEAWAYS

- Before you talk to brokers, banks, builders or developers, you need to make sure you are prepared.
- Get a broker who specialises in first home buyer finance.
- Too many finance applications can reduce your likelihood of getting a loan approved.
- To arrive at an unconditional finance approval, a bank will look at the buyer, the block and the building.
- When assessing the buyer, a bank will look at servicing potential, credit history, and deposit and costs requirements.
- Servicing is income versus expenses.
- Credit history is determined by your credit file.
- Banks will need to see enough savings to cover your deposit as well as costs.
- The bank approval you need is an unconditional approval.
- If you find you can't purchase a home right now, ask yourself how you can change your circumstances.
- For every problem, there is a solution.
- Stay positive. Be determined.

CHAPTER 4
Network

Just as it takes a village to raise a child, it is going to take a small army of people to help you get in to a home. It's time to assemble your team of experts. Just like in any industry, however, if you are not in the home buying industry all the time, living and breathing the current issues, it can be hard to know where to start or who to trust.

You are going to need a mentor to help guide you through the process. You will need access to blocks of land, land developers and land agents. You will need a builder to design and construct your home. You will need a broker to get your finance approved. Finally, you will need a solicitor or conveyancer to transfer the block in to your name. Who are all of these people? What do they do? What should you look for when selecting them?

In this chapter, I provide the fundamentals of who you will need in your corner, and outline some tips and tricks on finding the best people. I also offer some words of advice as to what to look out for.

Mentor

The right mentor who can guide you through the home purchasing process is the single most important person on your team. A good mentor is going to be able to push you at the right moment, support you when you feel like giving up, light the path for you to move forward and alert you to any hazards that lie ahead. A good mentor, however, can be very difficult to find. I think the biggest reason for this is when it comes to real estate everyone has an opinion – and most people think their opinion is the right one.

The truth of the matter is most people have very limited exposure to real estate transactions. The majority of people will make one or two transactions in their life, often spaced out by many years, sometimes decades. Whatever knowledge they do have is going to be limited to the street they live in and will often be decades old. People with the best of intentions can often create more problems than they do solutions. The worst bit is they can often be the most important people in our life – such as parents, uncles or aunties. It's not that they don't want the best for you – they definitely do – it's just they are so limited in their knowledge and experience that they're not really in a position to offer advice. Given it's such an important subject, it's difficult for people you care about to say, 'Actually, I don't really know what I'm doing.'

When looking for a mentor, you need someone with a proven track record. They should have a number of real estate transactions under their belt, and the transactions need to be recent. Buying a house now is a very different proposition to buying a home in 1990 or even 2010.

Their knowledge also needs to be specialised. You are attempting to buy your first home, and this is a very different proposition to buying your second home or an investment property. You are likely going to have your own unique set of circumstances that need to be addressed. You need to deal with someone who understands first home finance, deposit issues, construction, two-part contracts, house and land packages, and government grants.

Ideally, this person will have access to all of the industry connections you need. Rather than you having to go through the pain of trying to find the right builder, broker, developer and solicitor, they can give you a phone number, an introduction and a recommendation. This can save you hours of time and heartache.

Your mentor needs to be committed to you and available. Buying a home is not always a straight line, and the emotions you are going to experience will definitely be up and down. You are going to need someone who has the time and desire to help you through it – to support you when you need it and push you when you need it. You need someone who is prepared to go the extra mile and not give up on you. You need someone who will take your calls and answer your many questions.

It can be a tall order to find all of that in one person – and this is one of the main reasons I started my business. Our aim is to be that mentor for our clients.

Land developers and land considerations

If you've settled on building a new home, you are going to need a block of land – and the gatekeepers to the blocks are developers. Like people in all industries, you can get great land agents and not so great land agents. Rather than relying on the agent to find your ideal block of land, I think it's best you are proactive.

As discussed in chapter 2, once you have an idea of how much you can afford to spend on land, you can get yourself a list of developers by jumping online and Googling land in your preferred suburbs with a maximum budget in your price range. Do this weekly while you're deciding on your preferences, because blocks can sell quickly and the land market is an ever-changing landscape.

Before you call the developers you have identified as offering the land you're interested in, you are going to need a shopping list of the aspects you are looking for. The areas to consider in the following sections are not exhaustive, but they will give you a starting point as to what to look for.

Registration date

Let me give you a quick 'land developing 101'. Land developers purchase paddocks that they will then turn in to blocks of land. That whole process is going to generally take between three and five years to happen. This means developers want to sell their blocks as early as they possibly can, and will sell what are known as 'unregistered' blocks. Think of buying an unregistered block as similar to an off the plan land sale. You put your deposit down but you won't actually be able to complete the purchase until the land is 'registered' at the land titles office. When you purchase a block of land, the land title gets transferred from the developer's name in to your name.

You want to purchase land that is registered (titled) or just about to be registered – say, within three months. This is extremely important and I'll tell you why.

You'll sign a contract with the developer that is subject to finance. Once your finance is approved, you will need to waive your finance clause – making you 'unconditional' on the block of land. (The sale being 'unconditional' means you are now obligated to buy the block of land.) In the event you don't buy the block, the developer will keep your deposit and in the event they resell the block of land for less, they can sue you for the difference in price between your contract and the resale contract plus any costs such as interest.

Why wouldn't you purchase the block if you had your finance approved? Good question, and the answer reveals why registration dates are so important.

Your approval with your bank will have an expiry date. Some banks allow three months, others six months – it will depend on your lender. In the event registration blows out on the block for longer than your approval lasts, you will need to have your loan reapproved. Having your loan reapproved is not guaranteed. You may lose your job between now and then and all of sudden you no longer service. Interest rates may change between now and then and you no longer service. Or nothing external may have changed but the bank's lending policy may have changed between now and then and they now decline your loan. The developer doesn't care that you can't get reapproved and the lender doesn't care that you are unconditional on a contract. It's a disaster for you as a first home buyer because you are stuck with the consequences of circumstances you didn't create.

This is why I say ideally buy land that is already registered, which means as soon as you are approved you can book in for settlement. (Settlement is when the land transfers to your name.) In some cases, you may decide to go ahead if registration is three months away, but I wouldn't enter into a contract to purchase a block with registration any further than three months away. My thinking behind this is it will likely take you a month to get your finance approved, by which time land registration will only be eight or nine weeks away.

One other reason is important to note. Developers get their registration dates wrong all the time. Optimistic people would say this is because a lot of unknown circumstances can affect a land development – for example, if it rains, a lot of the civil construction cannot be completed and this will delay construction and, therefore, registration, which is outside the developer's control. A less generous person would say that land developers are overly enthusiastic in registration estimates or, worse, mislead customers – which happens to lead to more land sales for the agent. No-one will ever know the full truth but, as with most things in life, reality probably lies somewhere in the middle.

If registration is only two or three months away and all the civil works are completed, the only delays now will come from council. While significant delays can happen in council, they are less likely. You can also easily verify where the development is up to by going and looking with your own eyes – that is, are the streets in and is the guttering completed?

Case study: Beware the long registration date

A few years back a developer was selling land in a location that will remain unnamed. During the COVID property boom, the developer sold up the entire estate and told potential purchasers registration was six months away. Property prices soared during this time and the developer now told the purchasers registration was delayed, citing difficulty getting materials to complete the civil construction of the block as the reason. While this was certainly an issue experienced universally across the country during this period, there was also a lot of talk in the industry that the developer was deliberately delaying so he could ultimately invoke a sunset clause. (A sunset clause is a clause in a contract whereby if the property hasn't settled by a particular date either party may terminate the contract.)

Once the sunset clause could be activated, the developer went ahead and cancelled everyone's contract and refunded their deposits. The reason he did this was the cost of land had nearly doubled over the two years of first signing the contracts, and he wanted to resell those blocks at the higher price and make more money. It was a disaster for many of the people who had purchased in the estate because, while they could afford the original price when they signed the contract, property prices had now gone up by so much that they were now in a very difficult position. They were forced to pay more money for the same block or live in a suburb further away. Some people could no longer afford a property at all.

Avoid these issues completely by only buying land that is registered, or very close to being so.

Contract conditions

When you purchase a block of land, you will either sign an unconditional contract or a conditional contract. As already discussed in the previous section, when you are unconditional on a contract you are obligated to buy the block – and if you don't, you will lose your deposit among other consequences.

A conditional contract has conditions to the purchase listed. Many conditions can be included but the one you will need to utilise is what's called 'subject to finance'. Subject to finance means that, while you're willing to sign a contract with the land developer to buy the block of land, you need to get a loan approved to do so. In the event, you are unable to get finance for the block of land, you need to be able to exit the contract without penalty, without obligation and get your full deposit returned. The subject to finance clause of the contract will have a specified period – typically 21 to 28 days – during which you need to get your finance approved.

If a land developer won't let you include a subject to finance clause in the purchasing contract, I wouldn't deal with them. As covered in chapter 3, even with a loan pre-approval, you have no guarantee you will be able to settle on a particular block. Remember – the bank will consider the three Bs when approving a loan. The bank may decide they don't like the block of land or the building you are putting on it, and not grant you the full loan. Unconditional purchasing contracts pose too much risk to you, so always get a subject to finance clause added.

Deposits

Typically, a land developer will require an initial deposit and a balance deposit. When you purchase a block of land, quite often a developer will have you fill out and sign an expression of interest (EOI) form, which includes your basic details and the block details. When you sign the EOI, the developer will ask for an initial or a holding deposit. Developers do this because they want to make sure you are serious about purchasing the block – and so make you cough up some 'pain money'. From their point of view this is fair enough – a bit of work and expense goes in to preparing contracts, and money is the quickest way to gauge a person's intent. An initial deposit can be any amount but tends to be between $2000 and $10,000, depending on the developer.

The balance deposit will be due at a later date. A lot of developers will ask for the balance deposit to be paid on your finance approval, although some developers will ask for it to be paid a set number of days after the contract is signed. Provided you have a subject to finance clause, the developer is obligated to give all deposits back if you are declined finance during the finance period. A balance deposit is typically 5 or 10 per cent of the purchase price, but can be any amount.

The initial and balance deposit you pay will be included as part of your savings in what the bank calculates when they are looking at your deposit and costs.

Note that if you can't afford the deposit, you can't buy the block. If the land developer wants a 10 per cent deposit but you only have a 5 per cent deposit, that block may not be for you. Having said that, deposit conditions are negotiable. If a developer is asking for a 10 per cent balance deposit but you only have 5 per cent, you can ask them to alter their conditions to 5 per cent. No harm comes from asking – the worst they can do is say no but quite often, if you have a good reason, they will agree.

Land size

Land size can often be a bit misunderstood by first home buyers. People get an idea they need a particular size block without knowing what that size block actually looks like. Often the decision is made on the example of a friend who has told you their block size and you like the size of their yard. What a lot of people don't take in to consideration is the size of the friend's house in relation to the block, and also how much land is lost to the side of the house. Many people who want a bigger block are motivated by potential yard size, and fair enough. When you have kids and they need somewhere to play. However, you can often get the yard size you want on a smaller block.

Let me give you an example. One of our builders has a display home on quite a large block – 500-odd m^2. The block is quite wide but the house is not. What this means is much of the block is lost to the side of the house. Instead, we frequently put clients on 375 m^2

blocks and they end up having the same yard size because the land is used more efficiently.

The other thing to consider is your budget is likely to be limited for this first home purchase, so you often have to compromise. Perhaps you can have a monster block but you will need a smaller home or vice versa. Or you won't be able to live in your preferred suburb.

What I would definitely encourage you to do is to go to a vacant block of land that you believe is too small and walk to the back of it and then look at the block. I do this with clients all the time and when we stand at the back of the block and look at from this viewpoint, you realise how much land it is. I've had many a client who has gone for what they originally thought was too small a block after we go through this exercise. Have an idea of what size you'd like but make sure it's based in the reality of what you need and, most importantly, what you can afford.

Block shape

Traditionally shaped rectangle blocks are nearly always going to be the preference for buyers and builders. Blocks shaped like ninja stars may seem like a bargain but they're cheap because they are a disaster to build on. Your builder will often need to do a custom design, which you will need to pay for, and a lot of the extra land will still likely end up going to waste.

Occasionally, however, an odd-shaped block may work well. For example, I had a client who went for a block that was wide at the front and then tapered at the back. This allowed him to put a gate on the front fence so he could park his boat at the front of his house. We were still able to fit a standard design house on the block, which kept his costs down, and given the unusual shape of the block, it was slightly cheaper and, therefore, within his budget.

This was perfect for him and suited what he was looking for, but your safe bet is to look for a regular block.

Gradient

Gradient is the slope on the block. Sloped blocks tend to be very cheap, because they can cost a fortune to build on. You can find out the gradient of an unregistered block by asking for the disclosure plan, which will include contours showing the height of the block. Provided the drop from the highest point to the lowest point is less than one metre, you should be fine. You can often also just ask the agent if is the block has a slope or drop and they will tell you. You can also ask your builder to check out the block and let you know.

Covenants

Covenants are the rules developers have for their blocks of land. Covenant rules are generally made to keep estates looking beautiful, and can cover what materials you can use or even who can live in the property! This means covenant rulings can have an impact on the cost to build in estate, but they're not always a bad thing.

One of the estates we work with has very strict covenants, and clients need to spend on average about $10,000 more to build a house in the estate due to the rulings about materials, fencing and facades. They also have a rule that 90 per cent of all blocks must be purchased by owner occupiers rather than investors, and this is strictly enforced. This has led to the estate becoming a thriving community – because practically everyone who lives there owns their property, the neighbourhood has deep and lasting connections created by its community. This then leads to further demand, meaning the estate goes up in value and everyone wins. While it cost more to purchase in this estate, I think the pay-offs have definitely been worth it.

To find out more about potential covenants, tell your builder what block you want to buy and they can contact the developer on your behalf.

BAL and acoustics

BAL stands for Bushfire Attack Level and relates to a property's proximity to fire hazards and its likelihood of being hit by embers and flames in the event of a bushfire. The higher the BAL rating for the property, the more restrictions that will be in place on building materials and the more expensive it will be to build the house. Often a block with a high BAL rating will be cheaper to purchase because it's hard for the developers to sell due to the building costs being higher.

Acoustics ratings relate to the proximity of the house to noise, and how much of this noise can be heard within the house. A block of land close to a main road will likely have higher levels of potential external noise, meaning the house built on this land will need to be insulated from the noise – thereby increasing the costs of the building.

If you tell your builder which block you are looking at, they will be able to work all of this out on your behalf.

Flooding

In Queensland, most new estates are above the 'Q100' level, which is the 'one in one hundred year' flood level, so the potential for your property to be flooded is not something you need to worry about. If you are buying an urban infill block or a block in an established estate, potential for flooding may be a consideration. Again, the best bet is to get your builder to check out the block prior to purchasing.

Soil type

Soils are classified in to soil types such as A, S, M, H, E and P. Generally speaking soil types A, S and M are fine to build on, and soil types H, E and P may have restrictions and create additional costs to build on due to potential for movement from moisture or erosion. Rather than go into the specifics of these soil types here, again the best bet is to get your builder to look at the block you are hoping to build on and tell you about any additional costs.

Creating a shopping list for land developers

The preceding sections will help you build a shopping list of what you are looking for when talking to land agents. It's highly likely an agent will not have what you are looking for when you first call. Leave them your number and a shortlist of what you are after and ask them to call if something comes up. Don't leave it at that, however – the person who is most motivated to get this block of land is you so you need to push to get what you are after. Ring agents back once a week so you stay top of mind. Real estate agents constantly have finance falling over on blocks and blocks coming back on the market. They would much rather give that block to someone who is clearly keen – you – than deal with 336 online enquiries to get the same result. Provided your goals are realistic and affordable, this approach will eventually get you what you want.

A quick note on off-market sales. An estimated 20 per cent of all real estate transactions in Australia happen off market – that is, they're never listed online or advertised elsewhere. I have firsthand experience of this. My business has an extensive developer network with relationships we have forged for years. Before a developer has even turned the soil, they will meet with us, discuss their plans and, if we believe it is best for our clients, we will agree to take an allocation of blocks when they become available. These blocks never hit the open market. Unfortunately, for first home buyers this is a closed loop. The only way to access these off-market blocks is through the right mentor and network.

Builders

Building a home is awesome. You get to style and create something that is unique and truly yours. That said, building is not without its complications, especially for the uninitiated. In chapter 6 I provide a lot of detail on the building process, how to select a builder and what to look for. What I want you to keep in mind at this point is some notes on retail builders. If you've ever driven to a land estate and seen a display village of pimped out homes, what you are looking at is retail builders.

You've probably seen beautiful homes advertised on the internet for impossibly low prices. You may have even thought to yourself, *How can they build a home for that much?* I'll tell you a secret: they can't. What you are looking at is click bait, designed for the express purpose of getting you to click on the ad and drop deep in to the rabbit hole of retail builders.

The retail building model is structured like this. You go to their display home and get to walk through the 'Rolls Royce' of their available homes. The display homes are design masterpieces showcasing the full range of the builder's capabilities. They are seriously impressive – and completely unachievable for the average first home buyer. And while what they show you is the Rolls Royce, the pricing they give you is for the Holden Barina. Once you are committed to the builder and the purchase, you often then discover that everything you actually want in the home is an upgrade – and I mean everything. Even basics such as driveways and fences aren't included. It's not unusual to discover you have to add $50,000 or even $100,000 to the ticketed price to end up with the home you actually want.

Now I have nothing against retail builders; they definitely have their place in the world. If you are an established buyer with a bigger budget, a good idea of what you are doing and the ability to absorb extra costs, brilliant. If you are closer to your regular run of mill first home buyer, you likely have way too much going on already without having to worry about how you're going to get your driveway installed and which light fixtures are worth the money. It's simply too much.

My strong recommendation is to use a builder who offers you a full turnkey product, meaning everything is included. I also recommend you chose a builder who has a genuine fixed price build contract. (I go into a lot of detail about this in chapter 6).

Before you pick a builder, go and check out their display home, but the first question you should ask is, 'What in this building is an upgrade?' If the display home includes upgrades, ask how much it is to get the exact fixtures, fittings and inclusions that are in the home. Get the representative to point out all of the upgrades and then make a judgement call if you can imagine a house without the upgrades. If you feel you can't, then you probably can't make a decision on that builder because you don't really know what you're getting.

In my opinion, the sort of builder you want is the one who walks you through the home and says, 'This is the house. If you want this exact design, provided it fits on your block, you can have it. Nothing in here is an upgrade, it's all standard issue.' Walk around the home and picture yourself and your family in it. Can you see yourselves loving the home, can you picture dinners around the family table, kids playing out the back, you and your partner cooking in the kitchen and you all watching movies in the theatre room? If you can see it and feel it, it's probably the right place for you. If you get a little bit excited imagining your future, I reckon you're on to a winner.

Brokers

I talk about the importance of brokers when talking about getting finance ready in chapter 3, but brokers are so important that I think they're worth covering again.

The first home game begins and ends at finance. If you can't get finance, you can't get a home – it's as simple as that. And the biggest determining factor of whether or not you get finance is going to be the broker you chose. Don't go directly to a bank, because banking loyalty is misguided. If you want evidence of this, look at home loan rates. The cheapest loans for all the banks are offered to new customers. They quite deliberately charge existing customers more because they rely on customer loyalty and sometimes a bit of laziness to not change banks. Ultimately, they know they can get away with charging existing customers more and so make more money. They're not loyal to you, so don't be loyal to them.

The other reason I say don't go directly to a bank is because you are then dealing with one bank, which has one set of lending policies. (Lending policies are essentially rules as to when the bank will and won't lend.) If you don't fit that bank's mould precisely, you won't get a loan. If you go to a broker, however, that broker might have agreements with 35 different banks, which all have different lending criteria. It's logical that you will have a better chance of an approval with more banks to choose from.

Your broker must be an expert in first home house and land financing. You require a very specific and very niche type of loan. The degree of difficulty for the broker is high and the level of expertise required is substantial. Can other brokers secure first home loans? Of course they can, but if anything unusual jumps out at them they are likely to blame you rather than admit they don't know how to deal with the issue – or can't be bothered. I can't tell you the number of clients we have successfully got in to their first homes who have been told no elsewhere. It's not the broker's fault either – there is simply too much to know when it comes to first home lending.

Case study: Oscar and Melanie

In my business we have a team of brokers who actively workshop clients together every day. Loans that appear dead are resurrected all the time because of the skill-sharing expertise of the team.

A recent example of this was with two clients, Oscar and Melanie, who were earning excellent money but were in Australia on temporary visas. We searched high and low for a bank that would give them a loan on that visa, but everyone said no. It was very frustrating because they had a massive deposit, affordable goals and great income. The only sticking point was the visas.

We took the issue to our broker problem-solving session, and one of the brokers knew of one bank that would accept the application – literally one bank in the whole of Australia and we managed to find it. The only way you are going to get that from a mortgage broker is if they are living and breathing this type of lending every day.

Before locking in a broker, create a shortlist of brokers who you believe specialise in first home buyers and house and land finance.

Then call them all up and have a chat with them. Tell them your situation and your goals, and ask if they think they can help you. Ask them what they feel the limiting factors in your application are, and what financial support they can get you. Ask them about their experience in first home finance and house and land finance. Finally, ask them to tell you about a client like you they have helped previously, what their situation was, what they did to get them in to a home and what the outcome was.

By asking all of this, you should get a feel for the person. Do they feel genuine? Do they seem like they know what they're doing? The ultimate question you need to ask yourself is do you feel this person will go the extra mile for you? If the answer comes back as no or you're not sure, you probably haven't got the right broker. If the answer comes back yes, jump in feet first. Your broker is mission critical to your success.

Conveyancers or solicitors

When you purchase a block of land, the title of that land needs to be transferred from the developer's name in to your name under what's known as the Torrens title system. In order to get this to happen, your solicitor needs to talk to the developer's solicitor to facilitate the transfer. You can use either a lawyer or a conveyancer for this transfer – lawyers have broader expertise if something goes wrong, but conveyancers are cheaper for straightforward matters. For the rest of this section, I refer to conveyancers, but you can take this to mean either a conveyancer or solicitor.

If you are purchasing a house and land package, you will have a two-part contract: one contract for the block of land and one contract for the building. Your conveyancer is going to assist you with the land contract and land transfer.

The main thing to look out for with conveyancers is fixed fees. Some conveyancers charge extras for everything so, while they may seem cheap at first, once everything is added up they can cost quite a bit. An example of this is in the case of finance extensions. If you can't secure finance during the contract finance period, you will need to apply to the developer for what is called a 'finance extension'. Finance extensions extend the contract time allowed for you to get finance approved, and aren't unusual. Some conveyancers will charge for each finance extension, which you don't want – you want someone who is fixed price.

Conveyancers will also liaise with the bank prior to settlement to get the correct funds in place. These funds need to cover the deposit and all purchasing costs, and you need to have these funds available for the bank to settle on the land and put the property in your name. Believe it or not banks make mistakes with these calculations all the time. Given you only get this costing information one or two days before settlement, it can be a stressful time if any mistakes have been made. If your conveyancer is used to first home finance, including the first home owners grant, this is going to be helpful. If they already have a fantastic working relationship with your broker, this is even better. Your broker and conveyancer are going to need to work closely together to get the settlement of your property to go through.

To find a solicitor, ask your mentor or your broker if they have someone they would recommend.

Alternatively, search online for someone in your local area who does fixed price conveyancing, making sure you check their reviews.

KEY TAKEAWAYS

- You'll need to assemble a team of industry experts before finding and purchasing your first home.
- Ideally, your mentor will have specialised, recent knowledge and a network to leverage.
- Land you consider must be already registered or on schedule to be registered within three months.
- Make sure your land contract is subject to finance.
- Make sure you can afford the deposit.
- Put together a shopping list for your land.
- Stay in regular contact with developers and agents until you find a block.
- Get a fixed price full turnkey building contract.
- Ensure your broker is an expert in first home house and land financing.
- Ensure your conveyancer is fixed price.

CHAPTER 5
Support

A wise teacher once brought some balloons to school, told her pupils to each blow one up and write their name on it. After the children tossed their balloons into the hall, the teacher moved through the hall mixing them all up. The kids were given five minutes to find the balloon with their name on it, but though they searched frantically, no-one found their own balloon.

Then, the teacher told the children to take the balloon closest to them and give it to the person whose name was on it. In less than two minutes, everyone was holding their own balloon.

It's amazing what you can get done with a little bit of help.

This principle is behind the fourth of my first home foundations – Support.

The traditional route to home ownership was to live on oatmeal, beg borrow and steal to save for a deposit, and then give up a year of your life to real estate inspections – only to be outbid and outfoxed by cashed-up and more experienced purchasers.

If it was rough then, it's impossible now.

Here's why.

As discussed previously, the trend in real estate is for prices to go up, block sizes to reduce, and affordability to move outwards.

Our reality at the time of writing is interest rates have gone up, which means the amount you can borrow has gone down. At the same time, inflation has gone up, meaning the cost of living has gone up, pushing your capacity to save down.

For first home buyers, this is not good.

The time to save a deposit has blown out by impossible proportions. Here are the stats on how long it is taking the average Australian to save a deposit from Finder research:

- 36 per cent of first home buyers take five years
- 25 per cent of first home buyers take five to ten years
- 10 per cent of first home buyers take over ten years.

This means 71 per cent of the first home buyer market takes at least five years to save a deposit! In a property market that keeps rising.

I don't think I'm exaggerating when I say for most people this route to homeownership is pretty much impossible.

What should you do?

You need to find someone who has your balloon.

The 'balloon' in this circumstance is support. If you know where to look, a lot of support is out there for first home buyers. Mostly it's a matter of knowing where to look and what you're eligible for.

In this chapter I take you through the financial support that is available at the time of writing for first home buyers as well as the eligibility criteria. The information was correct when this book went to print; however, given a lot of the support is based on government policy, you should always check for any changes.

All the support discussed in this chapter assists with deposit and costs. The right support here can bring your dreams of owning a home forward by years. If you find something is else holding you back – for example, your income – check back to chapter 3 for some tips.

First home owners grant

The first home owner grant (FHOG) differs slightly state by state but many of the principles remain the same. Here I cover the Queensland first home owner grant. If you are in a different state or territory, check the relevant government website for further information.

The Queensland FHOG provides $15,000 towards your purchase. The grant is a gift from the government that you never need to pay back. They give it to you to assist you getting in to your first home (and in the hopes that you will continue to vote for them). Nearly all banks allow you to use the FHOG towards the deposit and cost you need to buy your home.

The grant is available for all Australia citizens and permanent residents over the age of 18 building a new home in Queensland. You must be building or buying a new home worth less than $750,000, including any contract variations. Existing homes are not eligible for the grant.

In some circumstances, if you are purchasing as a couple and one of you is a citizen or permanent resident and the other is not, you may still be eligible for the grant. New Zealanders living in Australia who are considered permanent residents are eligible for the grant. (Chur bro!)

If purchasing with your spouse, one of you may have received the FHOG previously while the other has not. This one is a bit of a pain, and we see a lot of clients in this situation. Unfortunately, if this is the case you are not eligible for the FHOG on the new purchase as a couple.

The grant is not available for investment properties. If you have previously owned investment properties but have never lived in them and never received the FHOG, you may still be eligible for the FHOG on your first owner-occupied purchase.

You must move into the property within one year of taking possession – that is, when it is built and ready to be lived in. You must live in the property as your primary place of residence for at least six months. You can rent out rooms as long as it doesn't affect your use of the home, although doing so may affect your eligibility for the first home vacant land concession covered in the next section. In relation to this, officials from the Queensland state government do proactively check if you are living in the home you have claimed the FHOG for, and if they find you have rented the place out they will come after you to get the grant repaid. Just as the book went to print it was announced the Queensland government has increased the FHOG to $30,000 until 2025.

The information provided here is not exhaustive but gives you the basics of the eligibility criteria. For further details go to the Queensland Revenue Office website:

First home vacant land concession

When you purchase a property, the government in the state or territory where the property is located will charge a tax known as transfer or stamp duty. Typically this tax is required at settlement, so you need to save it as part of your deposit and costs requirements for the property. Across Australia, states and territories offer discounts on this tax for first home buyers, so again check your relevant government website for further information. As a first home buyer in Queensland, you may be entitled to a discount on the transfer duty that can save you up to $7175.

To be eligible for the concession you must:

- be acquiring the property as an individual
- have never claimed the vacant land concession previously
- have never owned a residence in Australia or overseas
- be over 18 years of age
- be paying market value if the land is valued between $320,001 and $399,999
- build your first home on the land and move in within two years of settlement
- only build one home on the land
- not sell, transfer, lease or otherwise grant exclusive possession of all or part of the property before you move in.

To keep the benefit in full after you move, you must not sell the property within one year.

For a full listing of the eligibility criteria you can check the Queensland Revenue Office website:

First Home Guarantee

The First Home Guarantee is run by the National Housing Finance and Investment Corporation, which is a Commonwealth entity aimed at improving housing outcomes for Australia. Under the First Home Guarantee, you are able to purchase a home with a 5 per cent to 15 per cent deposit without paying lenders mortgage insurance. (As covered in chapter 3, lenders mortgage insurance is a fee the banks charge on loans with a deposit of less than 20 per cent.) It's not unusual for that insurance to be in excess of $20,000, and this fee needs to be paid up-front. This means it becomes part of the deposit and costs you will need to save. Being able to purchase a home without paying lenders mortgage insurance is a significant saving that has the potential to bring forward your first home purchase by years.

To be eligible for the First Home Guarantee you must be

- buying as an individual or a couple
- an Australian citizen or permanent resident at the time of entering the loan
- at least 18 years of age
- earning up to $125,000 for individuals or $200,000 for couples, as shown on your notice of assessment (accessible via your myGov account)
- intending to be owner occupiers of the home
- first home buyers who have not previously owned property before.

Property price caps are also included when accessing the First Home Guarantee. For Brisbane and surrounds, the maximum price is $700,000. You find the property price cap for all other areas here:

Properties that are eligible for the scheme include the following:
- a house and land package
- land with a separate contract to build a home
- an off the plan apartment or townhouse
- an existing townhouse, house or apartment.

The scheme is only available with 32 lenders. Your broker will need to ensure you meet the lending criteria for those particular lenders.

The deposit required for the lenders will vary but is generally between 5 per cent and 15 per cent. Depending on the bank's lending policy, those savings won't necessarily need to be genuine. For example, you may be able to use a gift from parents as well as the first home owners grant to make up the numbers.

The other benefit of the scheme is most banks will give you the same rates as if you had a 20 per cent deposit, meaning you will pay less interest.

Only limited allocations available with the banks are available through the scheme, but if you qualify it can be a great option. For full details or to access a calculator that will tell you whether you are eligible, use the following:

First home super saver scheme

The first home super saver (FHSS) scheme allows people to save money for their home by contributing pre-tax income to their super. This scheme offers a few benefits, with the first being you pay less tax on the money because it is within your super. As part of the income tax system, you're likely paying a marginal tax rate of either 32.5 per cent or 37 per cent, so reducing this down to the 15 per cent paid within super is a significant saving. The other benefit is you get investment earnings on that money while it's in super. You can only contribute a maximum of $15,000 per year and you can draw a maximum of $50,000 out, so you will need to plan well in advance if you are intending to use this scheme.

If purchasing the property with your spouse or partner, you can both have a FHSS going, which will hurry things up a little bit but it's still a long-term solution. Note that you cannot pull your employer contributions out of your super to purchase a home. This scheme is only for contributions you make beyond your employer's minimum contributions.

If you are a New Zealander now living in Australia and you have funds within the KiwiSaver scheme, I have some exciting news for you. You can move your KiwiSaver funds in to an eligible Australian super fund and then apply for the FHSS scheme and draw that money back out for your first home. Only a handful of Australian superannuation companies accept KiwiSaver transfers, but they do exist.

Check out all terms, conditions and qualification criteria for the FHSS scheme here:

Bank of Mum and Dad

Some lenders will allow you to use what are called 'non-genuine savings' – for example, funds gifted from your parents – provided you can still show proof of your ability to save. The policy varies from lender to lender; however, most banks work in the following way. The gift will likely need to come from a direct family member, although some banks allow the gifted funds to come from anywhere. The lender will want to see proof of your ability to save as evidenced by your rental ledger. You will need to be renting through a licenced real estate agent and be able to show six months' worth of payments where you have not fallen in to arrears.

So if you have a rental ledger available, shaking down the family tree and seeing if any money falls out might be worthwhile. Most people understand the difficultly first home buyers go through to get in to a home and if your family can see you are serious and responsible – and they have the means – they may be willing to help out.

Guarantor loan

If you have a strong income, a low deposit and a family member that wants to help you, a guarantor loan could be a great way to get into a property with little or no deposit.

When it comes to this Support element of my first home foundations, the guarantor loan is the premium solution for many first home buyers.

Let me explain why.

Understanding a guarantor loan and how it works

Saving a deposit can take forever! A guarantor loan is an option whereby you may not need a deposit at all. This is because, in a guarantor loan, 80 per cent of the purchase price is secured by your first home, and 20 per cent (the deposit amount) is secured by the guarantor's property.

The benefit of this includes the following:

- You may be able to get into your first home with a $0 deposit.
- You won't have to pay fees such as lenders mortgage insurance.
- A lot of banks will give you the same interest rates as if you had a 20 per cent deposit, meaning your loan repayments will be less.

What's the obligation of the guarantor?

The guarantor is not obligated to pay for any of the loan – you do that. In fact, if everything goes as it normally does, the guarantor has no obligation.

However, in the event you default on the loan, the guarantor is responsible for the 20 per cent component of the loan.

In practice, in the event of a default you would sell your property and then use the proceeds of the sale to pay off the loan. In the unlikely event that the proceeds did not cover the loan, the guarantor would need to cover the difference. At that point, everyone would be released of their guarantee.

How long does the guarantee last?

A guarantee lasts until you release it.

The most common method to release the guarantor is to wait for your property to go up in value and then move the security from 80 per cent your home and 20 per cent the guarantor's home to 100 per cent your home.

Who can go guarantor?

Most banks will want your guarantor to be a family member. The family member will need to have enough equity in their home to use as the guarantee.

If you have a strong income and a family member who is willing to help, a guarantor loan may be a way you can avoid spending years trying to save for a deposit.

Case study: David

A client of mine, David, came to us a little while ago wanting to purchase his first home. David earned great money working on the Brisbane Cross River rail project. His partner didn't work, staying at home to look after their two kids.

David had great borrowing capacity based on his servicing potential (income) but he had a low deposit, meaning he was limited by the $750,000 price cap for the first home owners grant. Given his lower deposit, we had to have that grant in order to get him in to a home.

During the Affordability (chapter 2) and Preparation (chapter 3) stages of the first home foundations process, we kept running in to a brick wall whereby the house David wanted cost more than $750,000. From a cash flow point of view, we were limited. In true 'stay positive, be determined' style we put our problem-solving hat on and workshopped solutions.

In discussing ways to get around the problem, it turned out David had a brother with equity who could go guarantor. Not all banks will allow a brother to guarantor – in fact, most want the guarantor to be a parent – so we went back to our brokers and workshopped lenders who would accept the brother as guarantor and found a solution.

Having the guarantor meant David was able to get the loan without a deposit, thereby eliminating the one problem that was holding us back.

KEY TAKEAWAYS

- The right support can bring your dream of owning a home forward by years.
- In Queensland, the first home owners grant is available to citizens and permanent residents if your purchase price is below $750,000.
- You need to live in the home for at least six months to be eligible for the first home owners grant.
- You will get a transfer duty discount via the Queensland state government if your block of land costs less than $400,000.
- The first home guarantee scheme is available if your purchase price is less than $700,000.

- The First Home Guarantee is available for couples earning less than $200,000 or singles earning less than $125,000.
- You can save up to $15,000 per year in to your super (to maximum of $50,000) to contribute to your first home deposit and costs.
- Some lenders may allow you to use a non-refundable gift for your deposit and costs provided you have proof of the ability to save via a rental ledger that is not in arrears for the previous six months.
- With a guarantor loan, it is possible to buy a home with little to no deposit.

CHAPTER 6
Build and style

This final foundation is where the fun begins. I take you through the practical steps of how to build a home that is unique and truly yours. I also discuss some of the common pitfalls and how to best to avoid them. Finally, I help you look toward the future for you and your family, really getting a feel for what owning a home means, how it changes you and the launching pad it can provide for the rest of your life.

This is my favourite step – where the rubber meets the road, where we create something that is strong, lasting and truly yours.

The ugly truth of living in rentals is deep down inside you know your house is not your own. You pretend to yourself that it's your home, but you know it's not. Nothing is permanent, nothing is yours. At any moment, you can have the rug pulled out from under you. At regular intervals you are reminded – the agent will want to inspect, your rent goes up, you can't have a dog or put a picture on the wall or, at worst, you may be evicted.

It's no way to live.

The future you dream of is a permanent base for your family, a community where you belong, long-lasting relationships with friends and neighbours, security, stability and pride of ownership.

This is the step where all of that happens.

Building a home will be one of the most rewarding experiences of your life. You will be able to take the vision you have for you and your family and turn it in to a reality. In this chapter, I take you through the basics of building a home, builder selection and how to craft a space that matches your family's lifestyle.

The building process

As covered in chapter 3, in order for a bank to give you an unconditional finance approval, they will assess the three Bs: the buyer, the block and the building. To begin with, you and your builder will need to settle on a design and a price. This design is not set in stone but you do need to go to the bank with a concept they can approve. Provided you are not making fundamental changes – for example, changing the slab and size of the house, or altering the number of bedrooms – you can move things around later on. A home is like a LEGO set – you can move a bedroom from the front of the house to the back of the house without creating a problem, provided the overall design stays on the same slab or footprint.

Generally, your builder will have 'off the shelf' designs that fit your block, are the right size house and have the correct attributes, such as four bedrooms, two bathrooms, a double garage and a separate media room. I suggest going with an off the shelf design so you can get your finance approval. If you go for a full custom design to begin with, the builder is understandably going to want to charge you to do that because if you don't get finance approved, they will have invested a lot of time and effort for no reward. If instead you go with an off the shelf design, the builder will generally provide the design and costings free of charge, which will allow you to get your finance approval with no financial risk. Provided you are remaining on the same slab with the same house attributes, you will be able to make changes later and the builder will be happy to do it because they are guaranteed you are going ahead with the build. Therefore, the first step in the building process is to pick a design, get contracts signed that are subject to finance and then head to the bank for an approval.

Once you have your loan approval and have gone unconditional on your contract, it is now time to meet your builder for your design and selections day. I find two types of people become apparent at this step. The first type of person wants it all done for them. They say, 'Give me a couple of colour schemes that have been preselected and matched, and I'll pick between those and then let's proceed.' The second type of person is the opposite, they want to sit down with a consultant and pick out every last detail that's going in to the house. They want to know what all their options are and then they want to mix and match so they can create something that is quite literally their unique creation. Funnily enough, if you are a couple you probably have one of each in the relationship. If you're the person who isn't fond of the detail, I have bad news for you: the person who loves the detail is going to make you sit through a full design and selection day! In my experience, builders will have a pathway for both types of customers. If picking every detail sounds like pulling teeth, they will have pre-selected colour palettes they can send to you. This means you don't even need to meet up with them, they can do it all electronically. If, however, you want to sit down with a designer, that option will be open to you as well. I go through some of the design and selection options later in this chapter.

Once you have finished with your design and selections, the builder will then apply for building approvals. The first approval will be covenant approval, which they need to get from the land developer. As discussed in chapter 4, land developers often have rules about how they want the homes to look and what elements such as facades (front of the house) need to be made out of. These rules are a good thing, because they will keep the estate looking great. Generally, builders will have no issues with covenant approvals, although I have seen people need to change aspects such as their external colour scheme because it was the same of the house next door. (Again, not a bad thing.)

Once you have your covenant approval, the builder will then go to council to get your building approval. Unfortunately councils work on 'government time' and may take anywhere from four to eight weeks to come back with an approval.

Once everything is approved, your builder will get cracking on your home. Build times can vary quite substantially between builders. Typically the build time for the builders we use will be between 15 and 24 weeks, although this can be affected by external unavoidable events, such as bad weather. I have heard a lot of horror stories with other builders about build times, so it pays to find out a builder's track record. (See later in this chapter for more on researching your builder.) In my experience, the builders who have the quickest build times are extremely systemised and process driven, while also having enough scale to ensure they are at the top of suppliers' priority list for delivering materials and trade.

The first step in the building process is base stage. The builder will prepare the block with site excavation and lay underground connections. They will then pour the concrete slab the house will be built on.

The second step of the building process is to put up the frame. This is where your building starts to come to life. All the rooms are marked out, the roof goes on and your home takes shape.

The third step in the building process is enclosed stage. At this stage, the home is at 'lock up'. All the walls and windows have been added and your home and the doors can be closed and the house locked up.

The fourth step in the building process is the fixing stage. At this stage, all the plasterboard and walls are completed, the cupboards are installed and the tiles are laid in your wet areas.

The fifth step is practical completion. At this stage, the home is, well, practically completed. A quality team will go through the home ensuring all work is completed to a high standard in preparation for handover.

The sixth step is handover. This is the day you have been waiting for – everything is done, and your hard work has paid off. Today, you get the keys and move in to your new home!

Full turnkey, fixed price

Building a home is an incredibly rewarding experience, but if you're not careful it can turn it to a very expensive experience. To ensure you avoid this, I recommend you deal with a builder who has a full turnkey product and offers a genuine fixed price construction. Let me explain why.

A full turnkey product means what it sounds like – you get the keys to your home and it's ready to be lived in, without any more money being spent. It's very common for retail builders not to provide this. As discussed in chapter 4, a common tactic is for retail builders to 'bait and switch'. They will advertise the lowest possible price, but with images or display homes with the highest possible specifications and inclusions. To give you a concrete price, they will often require you to pay a non-refundable deposit of $5,000 or more – and then once you are committed to the home and the builder, you discover that it's going to cost you a small fortune to get what you thought was included in the first place. I'm not saying they are lying to you; they're not. If you check the fine print on anything they have advertised or if you ask them, they will tell you elements such as driveways, fencing and landscaping aren't included in their basic price. However, this is often too confusing for someone who is just starting out.

Find a builder who has one price that includes everything with no hidden surprises. Things to check are included are driveways, fencing, landscaping and site costs. Site costs are the money the builder has to spend to make the block of land ready to build on. Quite often, for example, they need to do a site cut to make the block level and perhaps put in retaining walls if there is a slope. The costs of this can escalate quite quickly so you want to make sure they are included in your price.

The next is to ensure you have a fixed price building contract. A fixed price building contract is a contract that can't vary in price once the building has commenced. I can't tell you how important this is. At the time of writing, the building industry has gone through one of the biggest upheavals in most people's living memory. As I outline in chapter 1, during COVID the federal government released the HomeBuilder Grant, which gave home buyers $25,000 to use towards building their home. They did this because construction is one of the largest employers in the country and they wanted to keep the economy stimulated. They succeeded. The HomeBuilder Grant kicked off a massive boom in building contracts signed. Simultaneously, the COVID pandemic created a global supply chain problem. The demand for building supplies far outweighed the supply and the price of materials sky rocketed. In turn, the cost of building a standard four-bedroom house increased by $50,000 to $100,000 in a matter of months.

A further issue emerged. You may recall in chapter 4 I recommended only signing up for land that is either registered or a maximum of three months away from registration. A lot of people didn't do this. By the time their land was ready to be built on, the cost of building their home had sky rocketed. Builders starting sending contract variations to clients for $50,000 or $100,000 more – otherwise, they were told, they wouldn't build their home. (A contract variation is basically an unexpected bill.) It was carnage – a lot of deposits were lost and a lot of builders went broke.

Dangers such as these are still present in the market; however, they are reasonably easy to avoid if you ensure you do two things. First, do not sign up to land that is more than three months away from registration and, second, make sure you have a genuine fixed price contract. If you have a mentor, ask them to read over your build contract before you sign it.

How to research your builder

As already mentioned, the building industry can be a minefield for the uninitiated. When it comes to choosing a builder, a bit of research can pay dividends, and the one irrefutable source of truth when it comes to the building industry in Queensland is the Queensland Building and Construction Commission – or QBCC for short. (Other states and territories in Australia have similar but differently named regulators.)

The QBCC is the self-funded independent regulator of the building industry in Queensland. Builders pay a premium to the QBCC and the QBCC ensures proper building standards, and facilitates dispute resolution for defective building work.

You can also do a licence search on any builder you are looking to engage via the QBCC website:

Once you have found the builder through the licence search, you can then go to the licensee's full history. Here you can access a breakdown of how many builds the builder is licensed to complete per year and a record of their construction work year on year. Very often builders will imply that they are massive, completing hundreds of builds per year; when you look on the QBCC website, however, you may find they're more a 'mum and pop' show completing 10 builds a year.

Most importantly, the QBCC website provides a list of defective work, disciplinary action, infringement notices and demerit points recorded against a builder. This is where clients have gone to the QBCC to complain about the quality of past workmanship.

This information is invaluable when researching a builder. The QBCC will outline the nature of the complaint, if the builder rectified the work, and if any judgements or disciplinary actions were required. This means you can build a 'warts and all' history of the builder.

It's not unusual for the odd bit of defective work to be recorded that the builder needed to rectify but if you are seeing a history of poor workmanship and builder non-compliance, I would seriously reconsider engaging the builder.

Progress payments

A question I often get asked relates to when you actually start paying for your house. You will start paying interest on your loan as soon as you settle on the property but you do not make repayments based on the full loan amount. To begin with, your bank will have you on a construction loan. Construction loans are done via progress payments and are interest only. What this means is the loan is only drawn down based on where the construction is up to and you only pay the interest component rather than principle and interest. Again, you only do this during the construction period, which last a few months.

In the following table, I outline an example of the progress drawdown payments for a client, Tim, who bought a property in Flagstone (a suburb south of Brisbane). Tim was a single guy with one income so he was understandably stressed about trying to meet the interest repayments and his rent repayments at the same time. When we went through the actual numbers it became far less scary than he first thought. Because he was only paying the interest component and the full loan amount was slowly being drawn down, the initial repayments were quite low – until right at the end, which only lasts a few weeks.

Example loan repayments during construction

Land price	$202,000
Build price	$282,819
Package price	$484,819
Deposit	$48,482
Total loan	$436,337
Construction interest rate	4.66%

		Loan draw	Weekly repayments
Land		$153,518	$138
Deposit	5%	$167,659	$150
Base	15%	$210,082	$188
Frame	20%	$266,646	$239
Enclosed	25%	$337,350	$302
Fixing	20%	$393,914	$353
Practical completion	15%	$436,337	$391

As you can see, on day one Tim needed to pay for the land, and the loan was drawn down by that amount. Given Tim had paid a 10 per cent deposit, the loan for the land was only $153,518 and his repayments were $138 per week.

Next step was to pay the building deposit of 5 per cent, which draws down on the loan amount to $167,659 and makes his repayments now $150 per week.

Once the builder has laid the slab, Tim pays the slab payment, which makes the loan $210,082 and his repayments now $188 per week.

The progress-based drawdowns continue until the approved loan amount is fully drawn and you move in to your house. Once you move in, you switch to a regular home loan with principle and interest repayments.

Sometimes people make the comparison of not needing to cover loan repayments while still paying rent if you buy (and move straight into) an established home. Yes, they are correct but you also don't get the first home owner grant and need to pay a heap more in stamp duty. As covered in chapter 5, missing out on the combination of the two can often mean you end up having to save $25,000 or $30,000 more before you can get in to your home. That takes most people another two years, in which case property prices may have gone up another $70,000. You'll potentially end up costing yourself $100,000.

While the loan repayments on the progress payments are a little painful, they're often far less than what you expect and only last for a few months before you get your home. For most people, the pay-off of their own new home is worth it!

High-quality inclusions

The next thing you will want from your builder is to make sure they have high-quality inclusions as standard. If you are walking through a display home, make sure you ask what is included and what is an upgrade. As already mentioned, a lot of times you will discover the home you are looking at is nothing like the home you are paying for. I don't blame the builders for doing this; they're not set up for first home buyers and they are trying to show a cashed-up buyer what their capability is, which is fair enough. However, it's pretty confusing for you. If you feel like you can't understand what your house is going to look like when visiting a display home, it's probably not for you.

When you visit display homes, keep in mind that it's actually reasonably rare to be looking at the exact home you are going to have on your block. The reason for this is different blocks are going to be optimised for different styles of homes. What you do want to ensure is the basics of what you are seeing are the same – for example, even if the layout will be different, the size of the rooms will be similar and the fixtures, fittings and inclusions will be the same or similar.

It shouldn't cost a huge amount of money to get a great list of standard inclusions. Consider the following for your home:

- **600 × 600 floor tiles:** A lot of builders will use a smaller 450 × 450 tile. Unless you point it out, most people won't consciously notice the difference; however, a bigger floor tile will give you a different, more luxurious, feel for your home.

- **900mm appliances:** A 900-mm stovetop and oven is a must if you have a family. The oversized cooktop will make cooking dinner so much easier. Any builder worth their weight will have these included as standard.

- **Ceiling height:** A 2590-mm ceiling height is definitely a strong consideration. Some builders will include this as standard while others won't. If your budget allows for it, a higher ceiling height is a great inclusion. It gives a feeling of space throughout the home.

- **Ducted heating and air conditioning:** Some builders will include this while others won't. If ducted heating and air conditioning isn't included, it's an upgrade definitely worth considering. Otherwise, make sure the home comes with at least two split systems – one to the main living area and one to the master bedroom.

- **Epoxy garage floor:** An epoxy garage floor finish will give the floor a high-shine, high-end workshop finish while simultaneously helping you avoid the natural cracking you often see in garage floors.

- **Fans and lighting:** If you have a builder who is offering fan-lighting combos, run a mile. It looks cheap and nasty. What you want is downlights throughout the home and separate fans to all the bedrooms. Ideally, you'll be able to choose fashionable fans, such as a stainless steel look.

- **Floor to wall tiles in the bathroom:** If you budget allows it, seamless floor to ceiling tiles in your bathroom will give an amazing finish to your wet areas.

- **Oversized front door:** If the design of your house allows it, go for an oversized front door. It is not only practically a lot better, but also the first impression people will get of your home. Oversized doors give a feeling of grandeur.

- **Pendant lighting in the kitchen:** Two or three hanging lights over your kitchen bench look fantastic. If your builder doesn't include them as a standard, they are cheap to install and should definitely be a consideration.

- **Plush carpets:** A lot of builders include the 'rental range' of carpets as standard for a new build. This is the type of carpet you can graze a knee on and while it is perfect for rental properties because it will last a lifetime, it's not so great to live in. As a standard inclusion, look for a soft, plush, luxurious carpet. It will make a world of difference to the look and feel of your bedrooms.
- **Roller blinds:** I recommend choosing roller blinds over vertical blinds. Verticals are a pain, they don't block out the light and they break all the time.
- **Stone benchtops:** At a minimum, you should have stone benchtops in your kitchen and your bathrooms and you want the colours to match. Some builders will include waterfall stone bench tops in the kitchen, where the stone goes from the top to the floor. It's not a deal breaker but a lovely inclusion if you can get it.
- **Theatre room:** If you can afford it in your borrowing capacity, look at getting a house with a separate theatre/kids rumpus room. It's a great inclusion for your quality of life, particularly if you have kids. It gives parents – and kids – somewhere to escape to!
- **Tiled kitchen splashback:** The splashback wall behind your stove needs to be a fashionable finish. Tiles will give a good look and finish to your kitchen.
- **Walk-in pantry:** If your design allows it, I'm all about the walk-in pantry, particularly if you have a family.

You can do a lot with a home, and that's part of what makes building a new home so exciting. The preceding list should give you the basics of what to look for in your builder inclusions, and give you some low-cost ideas to give your home a finish that you and your family will love.

KEY TAKEAWAYS

- To get an unconditional finance approval, a bank will want to know what house you are building.
- Builders will often provide off the shelf designs free of charge.
- When you are approved, you will have a design and selection day.
- The building process is approvals, base, frame, enclosed, fixing, practical completion, handover.
- A full turnkey product has everything included.
- A fixed price building contract ensures no unexpected bills pop up.
- Repayments during construction are interest only with the loan amount drawdown via progress payments.
- Have a shortlist of high-quality inclusions you would like in the home.

CHAPTER 7

Looking towards the future

Congratulations! By now, you should have a solid understanding of the mechanics of buying your new home from start to finish. I now recommend going back to the start of the book and starting to put in to action the suggestions and recommendations. The first place to start is finding a mentor to assist you through the process. The right mentor will help you to move seamlessly from renter to homeowner. The world is a different place once you own your own home. Instead of living week to week and pay cheque to pay cheque, you can now look towards your future with an element of certainty.

In this chapter, I discuss the benefits and possibilities of the life you can choose to create for you and your family.

The emotional benefits of buying a home

My personal path to homeownership was to first buy investment properties before buying my first principle place of residence. The investment properties were amazing – buying them was a real achievement but the process was mostly academic. I didn't even go inside my first investment property. The property was in Adelaide, while I was living in Melbourne. Before I purchased it, I had never even been to the suburb the property was in. Only after I had got my loan approved and settled on the land did I go to see the block, and even then I was only there for a few minutes to take a couple of snaps and pat myself on the back for my achievement. For me, the purchase of that investment was fact-based. I considered whether the property would make money and the rent would cover the repayments, and whether it had the potential for solid capital growth (that is, the property increasing in value). To this day, I have never been inside that property and have no emotional connection to it. I felt it was a fantastic achievement but it was academic, like a box I needed to tick. While I was proud of that purchase, the feeling was nothing in comparison to the emotions I would feel when I bought my first house to live in.

To begin with, I applied a lot of the same investment thinking to my first home. I made sure the area I was looking at had potential for capital growth and there would be a good rental return if I decided to move out. I was quite detached. That all changed, however, the second I got the keys. I bought the house on my own and I was on my own when I first stepped in to it as the owner. I remember standing in the entrance and looking around in disbelief. I couldn't believe I owned it.

Despite all of my external achievements and experiences, inside I still felt like a kid. I couldn't believe that they had given me, a kid at heart, a house. I literally started laughing out loud by myself in the foyer of my first house. I walked around the house shaking my head in disbelief – it was mine; the whole thing was mine. Despite owning multiple properties by that point, it was the purchase of my first home that gave me the 'I've made it' moment. That feeling is the whole purpose of my business First Home Specialists. I want everyone to stand in the entrance of their own home, shaking their head and saying to themselves and/or their partner, 'I can't believe we did it.'

Owning a home changes everything. A strange psychological phenomenon is at play when you're in rental properties or boarding at your parents' house. Your life is categorised by insecurity and short-term thinking. I'm sure you've been through the experience (perhaps many times) where you've seen something around the rental property and thought you'd really like to change it – and then remembered it's not your house. When you get your own home, all of that changes. Instead of thinking in week and months, you start thinking in years. It changes your entire perspective of life for the better. As you begin to take ownership of your home, this then spills over in to all parts of your life. My experience is it changes you for the better.

On your way to meeting all your needs

I often talk about the typical home buyer journey, and I introduce this journey in chapter 1. As the following figure shows, the steps in the journey tend to be renting a property, buying your first home, buying your forever home and buying an investment home. Not everyone goes through all of the steps and not everyone does them in order, but they map out the typical home buying evolution.

I find as people move through these steps, a proportional security curve aligns with the steps. The more boxes you tick, the more secure you feel in yourself and your future.

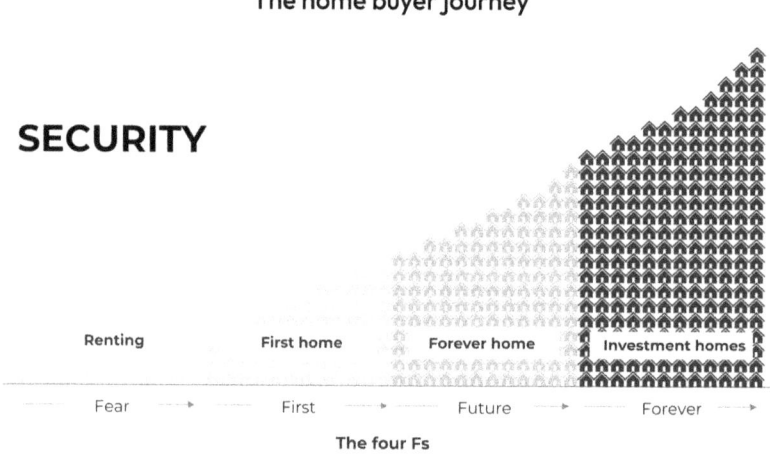

The home buyer journey

Abraham Maslow, a famous American psychologist, described this feeling of security – and the benefits that flow on from it – in what has come to be known as Maslow's hierarchy of needs (see following figure).

I believe the home buyer journey helps you move through each of the stages in Maslow's hierarchy. Your home gives you shelter, owning your home gives you personal security, being part of a community gives you love and belonging, owning investments and knowing your future is secure gives you status, strength and freedom. Once you have these needs covered you have the security, stability and freedom to become who you are supposed to be.

The purpose of this book isn't to take you all the way. The purpose of this book is to get you to take that all important first step.

If my experience and the experience of so many of the people I've worked with is anything to go by, the possibilities after that first step are mind-boggling.

Maslow's hierarchy of needs

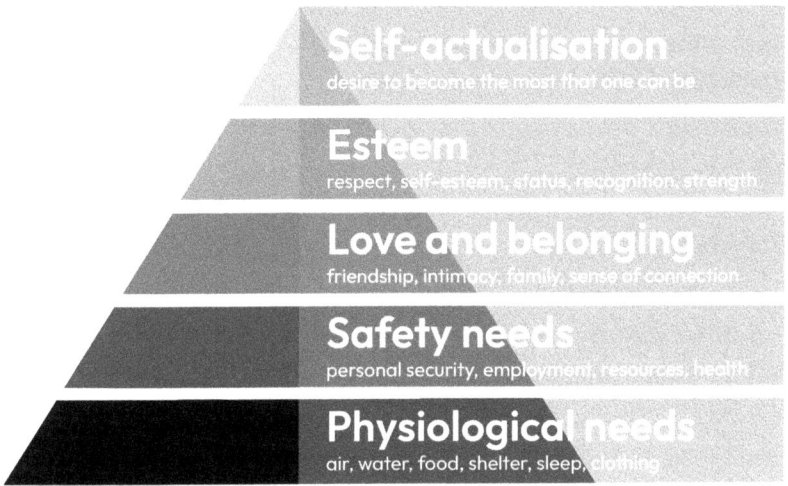

Leap frogging to your dream home

Most people's first home won't be their forever home. In fact, trying to buy your forever home as your first home is one of the biggest mistakes I see people make. This is the main reason the first principle in first home foundations is affordability. If your dreams are unrealistic or unaffordable they will remain just that – dreams. Back in chapter 2, I promised this didn't mean you couldn't have your forever home, but you would need to play the long game in order to get it.

Perhaps you've heard of a famous psychological experiment conducted by Stanford University back in 1972. The experiment was a study on delayed gratification, with researchers offering a child one small but immediate reward or two rewards if they waited a period of time. Researchers then left the child in the room with a single marshmallow or pretzel stick (the immediate reward, based on the child's preference) for 15 minutes. When they returned, if the child had not eaten the reward they were offered another marshmallow or a pretzel stick. Where this experiment gets interesting is in the long-term results. The researchers followed up with the children later in life, and what they discovered was the children who were able to delay gratification tended to have better life outcomes – as measured by SAT scores (it was an American experiment), educational attainment, body mass index (BMI) and other life measures.

If you are interested in the findings and applications from the marshmallow experiment for yourself or your kids you can check out The Marshmallow Test by Walter Mischel, the lead researcher in the original study. The available lessons, when learned and applied, can be life-changing.

This idea of delayed gratification reminds me of a famous quote from investment guru Warren Buffett: 'The stock market is a device for transferring money from the impatient to the patient.'

This has certainly played out in my life. When I was impulsive and living in the moment (which pretty well describes my twenties), I was unable to build anything lasting and of significance. The second I started playing the long game, my life started playing out in ways better than I ever possibly could have imagined.

Okay, so how does this play out with buying your dream home?

To buy your dream home, you are going to need to mix together a dose of reality and long-term thinking to get exactly what you want.

Let me show you how.

The first principle to understand is most people cannot save at the same rate that property goes up in value. Let me give you another example to demonstrate this.

Say you buy a house for $700,000 and the average detached dwelling annual growth rate is 7 per cent. In one year, $700,000 + 7 per cent = $749,000.

Your property has gone up $49,000 in value in one year!

Most people can't save that much in a year – in fact, you'd probably struggle to save that in five years. Whereas if you owned the property for five years, it would have gone up in value by over $250,000! This is called 'equity'. Equity is the value of your property minus the amount left on your loan. Whatever you have left over is your wealth tied up in the property.

Once you have the equity, you have two options to turn this in to your dream home. The first option is to sell the first home and use the proceeds to fund the purchase of your dream home. The second is to get an equity loan (a loan against the uplift in value of your property) and use these funds to purchase your dream home. The benefit of this is you will be able to keep your first home as an investment property and still buy your dream home. This is the best option if you have the ability to do so. You will have taken the first step in creating stability and security for yourself and your family, not only today but also well in to your future. Imagine if you were able to use the purchase of your first home as a stepping stone to securing your future in retirement and then creating generational security for your family. You could feel safe in the knowledge that when you leave this world your children or grandchildren will inherit property worth millions. For me, that's a legacy worth striving for.

The purpose of this book isn't to take you beyond your first home but if you structure that first purchase properly by following the first home foundation principles, the possibilities of what you can do from there are life-changing.

> **KEY TAKEAWAYS**
> - The first step in the homebuying journey is to find a mentor.
> - The security of owning your own home can change your life.
> - Your first home will likely not be your forever home.
> - You can use your first home to leap frog in to your forever home.
> - Play the long game.

Conclusion

Congratulations on making it to the end of the book. I hope I've opened your eyes as to what it takes to buy a home, the practical mechanics of how to go about it and the possibilities for you and your family in the future. Now you've got to the end, it's time to get practical. First of all, I recommend going back and completing the First Home Owner Scorecard for a second time. Comparing your before and after scores is a great exercise to help you see if you still have any knowledge gaps that need to be filled. If you do, flip to the relevant section of the book to skill up on the particular area. You should then have a clear idea of the overall picture of what you need to do to successfully purchase your first home, along with the common mistakes and areas to avoid. If you have decided you are ready and want to buy your first home, it's time to get started!

The most important person on your team is going to be your mentor. You will no doubt ask people for help during this process so take the time now to think forward and find the right person. Your best mate Robbo, while great to have a beer with and definitely steadfast in the convictions of his opinions, may not be the right person to entrust with the biggest financial purchase of your life so far.

The right mentor is going to have specific knowledge about your circumstances – for example, needing a low deposit loan, to buy a first home house and land package in South East Queensland. The knowledge needs to be based on recent experience, ideally in the last few months. If the mentor you choose has a pre-existing network of specialist brokers, builders, land developers and conveyancers, you can leverage this and save yourself hours of work and heartache. Most off all, you need to believe in and trust whomever it is you choose to get your advice from. If you're questioning their authority or motivations, or if you just don't really like them, this is going to be completely derail your first home purchase.

Trying to find someone with all of those attributes can be tough. I started my business First Home Specialists for exactly this reason. As a part of our process, we assign you a mentor who will take care of you from your initial phone call through to walking in your front door for the very first time. If you would like some help on your home buying journey you can contact us here:

I'd like to leave you with one final thought.

Buying your first home is in the top handful of experiences you will have in life. It is the true mark of your step into adulthood. It changes something in you. No longer are you at the behest of someone else, no longer is your life categorised by short-term thinking. Your first home is a source of pride, enjoyment, safety and security for you and your family.

A lot of people believe that their own home is out of reach. That it's an unachievable goal from a bygone era. Entire industries, such as build to rent, are being established to create and exploit a generation of renters.

It doesn't have to be that way.

Armed with the right knowledge and attitude, I believe a first home should be achievable for everyone.

As I outline in the introduction to this book, I'm on a mission to use First Home Foundations to create a revolution of first home buyers in Australia. My vision for the future is that the great Australian dream is kept alive for you, your children and every generation that follows.

Until we meet again.

Stay positive. Be determined.

Let's build memories in a home you love.

Leigh

Acknowledgements

Writing this book has been an amazing experience and none of it would have been possible without some help from amazing friends and clients.

To my best mate and business partner, Aaron. Who would have thought when we sat down in a café to map this out all those years ago, we would end up where we are now? And to think this is only just the beginning.

My 'work wife' Kali, you are the glue that holds the whole ship together, and your dedication and loyalty to the cause have been there right from the day this was just an idea.

My friends Rach and Pep, thank you for believing in me right from the very start, you have helped me to become the version of me that you always believed I was.

My cousin Elka, thank you for being my sounding board and for giving me unfettered support and feedback.

Tommy, thank you for your feedback on the book but more so for your friendship and support in the business world. You set a high standard for our clients and it pushes me to become better.

Juanito, your feedback on the initial drafts of this book were next level. This book wouldn't be what it is without the help you gave me.

Peter, I know you unwittingly got roped in to the editing process by Rachel and I appreciate the help you gave me – and that you did it all with a smile.

Cpaz, thank you for your thoughts on finance and for being a sounding board for me and our clients.

J-Dog, your tireless work on editing and production has been amazing.

Finally, to all of our wonderful customers, making your dreams come true has been one of the greatest honours of my life. You teach me as much as I teach you, thank you.

www.ingramcontent.com/pod-product-compliance
Lightning Source LLC
Chambersburg PA
CBHW041317110526
44591CB00021B/2816